REVIVING WORK ETHIC

A LEADER'S GUIDE TO
ENDING ENTITLEMENT AND
RESTORING PRIDE IN
THE EMERGING WORKFORCE

ERIC CHESTER

GREENLEAF
BOOK GROUP PRESS

Published by Greenleaf Book Group Press
Austin, Texas
www.gbgpress.com

Distributed by Greenleaf Book Group LLC

For ordering information or special discounts for bulk purchases, please contact Greenleaf Book Group LLC at PO Box 91869, Austin, TX 78709, 512.891.6100.

Design and composition by Greenleaf Book Group LLC
and Bumpy Design
Cover design by Greenleaf Book Group LLC
Cover photo by Eric Weber

Publisher's Cataloging-In-Publication Data
(Prepared by The Donohue Group, Inc.)
Chester, Eric.
   Reviving work ethic : a leader's guide to ending entitlement and restoring pride in the emerging workforce / Eric Chester. — 1st ed.
     p. ; cm.
   ISBN: 978-1-60832-242-8
   1. Work ethic. 2. Employee motivation. 3. Intergenerational relations. I. Title.
HD4905 .C54 2012
306.361/3   2011932963

Part of the Tree Neutral® program, which offsets the number of trees consumed in the production and printing of this book by taking proactive steps, such as planting trees in direct proportion to the number of trees used: www.treeneutral.com

Printed in the United States of America on acid-free paper

11 12 13 14 15 16   10 9 8 7 6 5 4 3 2 1

First Edition

CONTENTS

■ ■ ■

Acknowledgments

I owe my work ethic to my father, W. Grant Chester, whose mission in life was to make certain that his only son knew how to survive—and succeed—in any economy. Thanks for teaching me how to work, Dad, and for convincing me to never sign my name to anything that wasn't my very best effort. I wish you were alive to read this book; your fingerprints are all over it.

I owe a huge debt of gratitude to several very close friends and colleagues for encouraging me to tackle this difficult topic, hit it hard, pull no punches, and stay on task. Thanks to Mark Sanborn, Theo Androus, Dan Thurmon, Chase LeBlanc, Shep Hyken, my attorney—Jeff Brimer of Faegre & Benson—and to my wise-beyond-his-years son-in-law, Christopher Rhyme, JD.

I am fortunate to be surrounded with great business partners who allow me to dream out loud and work tirelessly to bring those dreams to fruition. Thanks to my sister, Christie Michelle, and also to Matt Smith, Tom Kilijanek, PhD, Fred Waugh, and Seth Ford.

A huge shout-out to the following very gifted writers for helping me craft my ideas and put them on paper in a logical and compelling way: Stephen Caldwell, T.J. Wihera, and my son, Zachary Chester.

Special thanks to my wife, Lori. No one works harder, cheers louder, and loves deeper.

■ ■ ■

Foreword

When Eric Chester asked me to write the foreword for *Reviving Work Ethic*, I was thrilled. Not just because I love to read Eric's books, but also because the subject of this new book—handling and being handled by the next generation—is such a fascinating and critical topic today!

How do you develop work ethic in the emerging workforce? Better yet, how do you do that while building your own business? The solution, which Eric so eloquently provides in the pages that follow, is the key to the success of both those in leadership positions now and those to whom the baton of leadership will be passed.

With all the changes happening in the world today, young people just entering the workforce in the West will be working in an atmosphere that is completely different from the one previous generations entered into.

The hard fact is, it's tough out there, and it's only going to get tougher. In the past, older people have historically liked to brag: "When I was young, things were tougher." I don't believe this is accurate anymore. I say, "When I was young, things were easier."

For one thing, we have globalization. Lots of us thought globalization meant that people around the world would be competing to buy our products. What we're finding is that it often means people across the planet are competing for our jobs. Millions of smart, hardworking young people—who speak fluent English—are graduating from colleges around the world. Many of them have no expectations of being handed anything. They know they are going to have to make it based on their own motivation and abilities.

In today's era of uncertainty, nothing can be taken for granted. Young people need to develop skills and talents that will make them globally competitive. They need a strong work ethic to survive and thrive. And Eric's point—that if you develop this work ethic, you will strengthen and build your own business—could not be more pertinent.

No matter what industry you work in, this book will be useful to you and the young people you are striving to help. Read it and you, too, will understand how developing work ethic in the emerging workforce will build your business *and* launch their careers!

—Marshall Goldsmith, world-renowned executive coach and author of the *New York Times* bestsellers *Mojo* and *What Got You Here Won't Get You There*

■ ■ ■

PROLOGUE

The decline of work ethic is not uniquely an American problem, but one that is affecting all Western nations and a growing number of those in the East.

Further, the lack of work ethic is not a problem that can be attributed to any specific demographic or generation. However, the ideas and strategies for reviving work ethic that follow are more easily applied—and the overall impact is more sustainable—with teens and young adults, as these individuals' workplace habits and core values are still being formed.

This is a battle no organization or country can afford to lose, much less continue to ignore.

■ ■ ■

INTRODUCTION

Imagine that you are walking alone across a vacant parking lot on a breezy day, when out of the corner of your eye you notice a crumpled-up bill blowing at your feet. You immediately step on it to keep it from escaping, and then reach down to discover that it's a $100 bill.

No one is within five hundred yards of you, and the wind is swirling leaves and other bits of paper around as far as you can see. You couldn't find the rightful owner if your life depended on it. The bill is yours to keep.

Thinking only of your emotions as they unfold at that particular moment, allow me to ask you a very simple question:

Are you happy?

Of course you are. Unless you're allergic to large bills, your response was an enthusiastic "yes!"

So here's the follow-up question pertaining solely to this $100 cash windfall moment:

Are you proud?

Unless you're overthinking this, you're probably shaking your head or thinking, "No, not really." You're happy about your new riches, but you're not particularly proud.

You didn't do anything to earn this free money other than burn a calorie or two bending down to pick it up.

In this scenario, there was no goal, no effort, no sacrifice, no accomplishment . . . nothing to be proud of.

Getting something for nothing isn't bad, or evil, or immoral. Who doesn't appreciate a little good fortune coming their way? However, when finding ways to separate effort from reward becomes a passionate pursuit, any treasure obtained in the process is marginalized. There is no enduring joy without pride, and pride cannot be realized without contribution.

The *New Oxford American Dictionary* defines the word *proud* as "feeling deep pleasure or satisfaction as a result of one's own achievements, qualities, or possessions or those of someone with whom one is closely associated."

This is a great definition, but I think that the sequence of the nouns *achievements* and *qualities* needs to be reversed. A person's *qualities* lay the foundation for his or her *achievements*. It's hard to achieve anything worthy of merit without demonstrating qualities like reliability, determination, perseverance, and integrity. And while *possessions* can make you happy, they won't make your chest swell with pride if they've blown into your life without achievement.

There was a time when achievement meant more than possessions, and when character (a person's qualities) was valued more than achievement. Americans felt good about putting in an honest day's work for an honest day's pay. This was the time when "Made in America" was the best label any product could bear, quality was everyone's priority, and companies made decisions to ensure long-term stability—not short-term gains for stockholders.

I'm north of fifty and I remember that time. My four children (ages twenty-six to thirty-one) don't.

They've grown up in a world where most people work hard to find ways of avoiding hard work. They've heard stories telling how lottery winners, day traders, bloggers, dot-commers, and Internet marketers have managed to beat the system and derive a huge bounty with little or no effort. They've been inundated with reality television that turns talentless fools into millionaires in the blink of an eye and with the greatest of ease. To them, an apprentice is not a young worker learning a trade at the foot of a master craftsman, but rather a devious schemer finagling to get a coworker fired by Donald Trump. Not surprisingly, *The 4-Hour Workweek* is more than a national bestselling book; it's a rallying cry.

Is it any wonder there is a burgeoning entitlement mentality among the new workforce?

Work has degenerated to little more than a four letter word; a necessary evil. It's no longer viewed as something to be proud of, but rather something to disdain, to shortcut, or to elude all together. (Thankfully Franklin, Edison, Carver, Bell, Ford, Einstein, Salk, Disney, Gates, Winfrey, Jobs, and Zuckerberg didn't see it that way.) If we do nothing to reverse this gross misconception, we will not only be doing our kids a great disservice; we will be allowing the further contamination of our labor pool.

Leaders can no longer stand by idly in hope that parents and teachers will resume the responsibility for instilling work ethic. Parents now focus most of their attention on ensuring that their kids are healthy, happy, and have a high self-esteem. Meanwhile, schools are facing widespread criticism and massive cutbacks, and are concentrating every available resource on increasing test scores and keeping students safe.

Therefore, the burden of developing work ethic within the emerging workforce has shifted to employers. Organizations that neglect this responsibility will continue to point the finger at parents and schools for the unsatisfactory product they are getting. They'll have no choice but to export labor overseas, replace human interaction with touchscreen technologies, or churn-and-burn their frontline people, whom they see as an expendable commodity.

Leaders that accept this new reality and rise to the challenge will create cultures that promote the qualities and values described in the pages that follow. In so doing, they will develop talent pools that soon run deep with creative, energetic, and dedicated individuals whose efforts boldly exclaim, "I'm proud of my work."

It's time to revive work ethic.

■ ■ ■

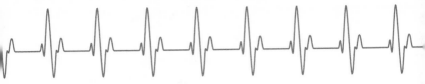

CHAPTER 1

REWINDING THE GAME OF LIFE

Abraham Lincoln's decision to grow a beard back in 1860 delivered an unintended but life-changing blow to a young entrepreneur in Springfield, Massachusetts.

A portrait of the presidential candidate started out as a hot seller for the self-taught lithographer and printer. But then an eleven-year-old girl wrote Lincoln a letter suggesting that his face looked too thin and that a beard might help his chances at the ballot box. As a result, Lincoln avoided the barber for a few weeks, sprouted a full face of whiskers, and created the iconic image that we now see when envisioning the sixteenth president of the United States.

Undaunted by the sudden decline in demand for images of a beardless Lincoln, the young entrepreneur drew upon his hardscrabble roots and moved forward. With winter approaching, Milton Bradley put his imagination to the grindstone and came up with something new.

He called it The Checkered Game of Life.

Bradley's game, set up on a board that mirrored a standard checkerboard, took players from a starting square labeled "Infancy" to a square in the farthest corner labeled "Happy Old Age." Since dice still carried the stigma of gambling, the players advanced or regressed based on the spin of a teetotum—a top with numbers. Players collected points and moved forward when they hit squares for virtues such as bravery, honesty, and perseverance, but they also were rewarded for landing in the "fat office," going to college, getting elected to Congress, and accumulating wealth. Setbacks resulted from landing in poverty or prison, or from negative virtues such as idleness, intemperance, or gambling.

Due in part to the Industrial Revolution and the American frontier spirit, virtues had come to be regarded not just as ends in themselves, but as means to advancement. Bradley made the connection between hard work, character, and business success. Players who landed on "Idleness," for example, had to move backward, while landing on "Honor" helped you move forward. Unlike the European caste system that rewarded fortunate bloodlines, The Checkered Game of Life taught and reinforced the idea that hard work and virtuous living provided anyone an opportunity for advancement and wealth.

Bradley, the son of a craftsman and the product of an industrial mill town in Maine, believed in and lived out these work ethic values, and he wanted to share them with the youth of America. He personally sold several hundred copies of The Checkered Game of Life within a few days of creating it and more than 45,000 within the first year, launching his career, as well as the entire board game industry. The Milton Bradley Company became synonymous with board games, and its founder became a member of the National Toy Hall of Fame.

It's a New Game

One hundred years after Bradley debuted The Checkered Game of Life, America had survived the Civil War, tamed the West, proven herself in two World Wars, and lived through the Great Depression. Eighteen presidents had followed Lincoln to the Oval Office. Rock 'n' roll had burst onto the scene, and the country found itself heading into the uncharted waters of the turbulent 1960s, with Vietnam and the assassinations of John F. Kennedy and Martin Luther King just around the corner.

The Checkered Game of Life, meanwhile, underwent a rebirth that mirrored the culture around it. To mark the hundredth anniversary of Bradley's original version, the Milton Bradley Company commissioned Reuben Klamer to create The Game of Life. Klamer's adaptation, released in 1960, replaced "Happy Old Age" with a new objective: "Millionaire Acres." The checkerboard became a winding road, and the game piece became a car with pegs that represented the player and his family members.

Each decade that followed brought new updates that continued to shift the focus away from virtues and toward materialistic rewards; players got ahead not by avoiding crime and laziness, but by being lucky. By the 1970s and 1980s, the game had added "share the wealth" cards that allowed players to collect part of another player's payday or required an opponent to pay part of his taxes. And if a player married or had a child in the game, mandatory gifts were in order. "Lucky Day" spaces provided an instant lottery-like windfall with an option to multiply it (or lose it all) based on a spin of a wheel (sounds a lot like gambling, doesn't it?). By 2010, the online product description of the game provided this as the objective: "Do whatever it takes to retire in style with the most wealth at the end of the game."

In less than 150 years, the game had shifted away from a focus on the rewards of social virtues, a strong work ethic, and adding substantive value to the community; it now focused on rewards, rewards, rewards. Even when the 1990s versions added incentives for community service activities like recycling or helping the homeless, there remained no mention of work or the ethos that underpins success. Careers were merely assigned a salary, and with that, a player could reap even greater advantages from gambling and the misfortunes of others—almost a 180-degree shift from Bradley's original version.

The game went from providing essential lessons on virtuous work ethic to being a model for achieving something for nothing. And in many ways, the transition of The Checkered Game of Life of the 1860s to the modern Game of Life pretty much mirrors the real-life changes of the last century.

The Current State of Work Ethic

Somewhere along the way, Western culture has lost sight of the virtues that comprise work ethic—the very things that helped build our country. The pursuit of happiness and the American Dream drove progress and innovation, but they came with unintended side effects. In many cases, for instance, healthy ambition has morphed into avarice. Urbanization and an emphasis on large-scale businesses means fewer and fewer kids are learning about work in the natural course of family life. Technological advances that make life faster, more fun, more entertaining, and easier to navigate are also consuming our time and energy while eliminating avenues for learning vital concepts about work. And pop psychologists have pushed parents to focus on building self-esteem in their children, creating at least two generations of me-centric workers. The goal, as rockers Dire Straits famously and bluntly sang in the mid-1980s, has become to "get your money for nothing and your chicks for free."

America's emerging workforce—those in the sixteen-to-twenty-four age bracket—finds itself uniquely positioned to turn this tide, both because of its size (fifty million by some estimations) and because the young are the most moldable. A transformation back to traditional work ethic—or at the very least an introduction to a traditional work ethic—within this age group will last for decades and influence the workforce and communities in positive ways for generations.

These workers bring some amazing skill sets and personality traits into the labor pool. In February 2010, the Pew Research Center released an extensive report titled "Millennials: A Portrait of Generation Next" that describes this generation (ages eighteen to twenty-nine) as "confident, self-expressive, liberal, upbeat, and open to change." It is history's first "always connected" generation, the report says, and it's on track to becoming the "most educated generation in American history."

But this generation doesn't identify with work ethic. The Pew research found that 61 percent of Millennials say their generation has a "unique and distinctive identity." That's about the same percentage you'll find for other generations, but what's different are the things Gen Y sees as its distinctive qualities.

In an open-ended follow-up question—"What makes your generation unique?"—work ethic was mentioned as a distinctive characteristic by at least 10 percent in the three older generations—Gen X (ages thirty to forty-five), Baby Boomers (ages forty-six to sixty-four), and the Silent Generation (ages sixty-five and up). That put it among the top five responses for those generations, and it was number one for Baby Boomers. It didn't make the list for Millennials. Millennials said that what made them unique was technology use, music/pop culture, liberal/tolerant beliefs, greater intelligence, and clothes.

All too often, these bright and ambitious recruits see work as something to avoid or as a necessary evil to endure prior to winning the lottery, landing a spot on a reality television show, or getting a cushy, high-paying job with a corner office and an expense account.

This presents a variety of challenges for those who desire to help young Americans get back to work. For starters, Millennials don't always want to work. And when they do, their terms don't always line up with those of their employers. All too often, the young worker shows up ten minutes late wearing flip-flops, pajama bottoms, and a T-shirt that says "My inner child is a nasty bastard."

Then she fidgets through her shift until things slow down enough that she can text her friends or update her Facebook page from her smartphone.

The Root of the Entitlement Mentality

Baby Boomers are celebrated for being hard workers. Many brag about the long hours they put in and how they work around the clock. To justify these workaholic tendencies, the common rationale is "I want to provide the best life possible for my children and give them what I never had." In Boomer speak, that translates to much more than providing a nice home, good health care, square meals, and a quality education; it means giving their kids the latest and greatest of everything under the sun. Showering their kids with material stuff not only makes parents feel like their children are keeping pace with the Joneses, but also helps absolve them of the guilt of not giving the children the personal face time they need—something that was lost during the long hours the parents spent working.

Numerous CEOs of major corporations have pulled me aside after a speech and made a confession: "My kids are far lazier than I was at their age." (It's as if they want some advice on how to get them motivated to work.)

After speaking at an executive leadership conference attended by the top CEOs in

According to an MTV study of 2,000 young adults ages 14–24, 71 percent of Millennials agree they are "too talented to punch a clock or sit in a cubicle."

the franchise community, Aslam Khan approached me with his cell phone in hand. He had dialed home to speak with his twelve-year-old son, Abraham, and wanted me to talk to him. Aslam came to America from Pakistan at age thirty, completely broke and not able to speak any English. In twenty-three years, he had worked his way from a dishwasher at Church's Chicken to the franchise's largest owner, with 153 locations and more than $100 million in annual sales. Aslam was obviously concerned that his son's work ethic wasn't as strong as his own, and he thought by spending a few minutes on the phone with Abraham, I could turn the lights on for him.

I didn't need to talk to Abraham to know why Aslam felt frustrated. Through his tireless work, he had created the kind of childhood for his son that he, himself, never had. Abraham is a bright, well-adjusted boy who does well in school, but Aslam didn't understand why his son did not inherit his work ethic. But with the privileged life Abraham is living, how could he?

This is a common tale with entrepreneurs and business executives who tell me how hard they had it when they grew up, and, in contrast, how many times their kids have been to Disneyland or gone on exotic cruises, how many pairs of $100 sneakers they have, etc. "They don't know how hard I've worked for all that stuff," the concerned parent tells me.

Of course they don't. The kid is just used to all those things being handed to him. In other words, he feels entitled to what his parents have provided for him. This is by no means a tale limited to wealthy business owners and executives; it's also commonplace when talking to engineers, small business owners, teachers, plumbers, and just about everyone else who grew up having to either earn what they wanted or do without.

Fame and Fortune As an Expectation

It's no coincidence that reality television and the emerging workforce came of age at the same time. With each feeding off the other, they give credibility to Andy Warhol's famous prediction that "everyone will be world-famous for fifteen minutes."

The teen dream of becoming a star—a rock star, a movie star, a football star, an Internet star, a reality-television star—is now more of an entitlement than an aspiration. The question for many people today isn't so much *whether* they'll get their fifteen minutes of fame as *when* they'll get it and what they'll do with it.

In the past, prominence came mainly through high achievement. To attain fame, you had to become the best of the best—the best actor, the best baseball player, the best scientist, the best writer, the best artist, the best politician, the best businessperson, or even the best outlaw.

Now, with hundreds of television and Internet channels begging for content, anyone can become famous for doing something incredibly bizarre, dangerous, weird, or self-deprecating. The bar to fame rests very low, and respect and admiration seldom enter the conversation.

Our culture cultivates this entitlement mentality early on by steering children toward the talents that the world values—signing, dancing, acting, athletics. We have good intentions, of course. If we have a prodigy on our hands, we want to find out early and nurture her so she can realize her full potential. What if little Nicky really is the next Peyton Manning, or if little Brooke is the next Miley Cyrus?

But parents, coaches, teachers, and other leaders of young people get caught up in the fame and lose our balance when we don't also teach them the skills and the follow-through that come with less glamorous labor—mowing lawns, waiting tables, prepping and painting a wall, washing clothes, keeping a room clean.

Some kids are pushed too hard and too fast; they work endless hours to become stars and end up burning out. But they are the exceptions. Less obvious—but living in just as much danger—are the ones who absorb mountains of praise without any foundation other than a sense of entitlement. Many of the brightest stars flame out all too quickly, not because they worked too hard but because they lacked real work ethic. A few—Manning for instance—shine brightly for years and years precisely because they learned these values early and had them reinforced often while growing up.

OD-ing on Self-Esteem

Many of the negative habits, mindsets, and attitudes embedded in the emerging workforce result from messages that have focused mostly on how great young people are and how they are special enough to warrant success, fame, and wealth without having to sacrifice much to get it.

In fact, two generations and counting have now been

raised on an overdose of self-esteem. For years, the cultural elite preached this message ad nauseum—praise and reward, praise and reward, praise and reward—with the overt goal of building self-esteem so that everyone feels valued, everyone wins, and everyone can see themselves as the best of the

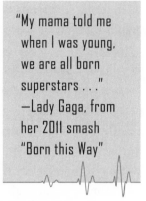

"My mama told me when I was young, we are all born superstars . . ."
—Lady Gaga, from her 2011 smash "Born this Way"

best. In varying degrees and in differing forms, this message emanates from all five areas that influence an adolescent's view of himself and the world: parents, teachers, peers, media, and spiritual beliefs.

Fostering positive self-esteem seems pretty good on the surface; it's much better than promoting self-loathing, right? But the heart of the self-esteem message is to *esteem the self*, and eventually that creates a self-focused, entitled mentality. Self-esteem can easily trump self-control and selflessness, and it's very different from healthy self-confidence or self-respect. So while the emerging workforce has been taught the importance of saving the world, these individuals also feel empowered to do so strictly on their own terms. They can quickly change course and move away from the most high-minded agenda if it isn't meeting their personal, self-established needs.

Naturally, this mentality—esteem for self over others—finds its way into the workforce as a lack of respect for anything that doesn't please and satisfy the young employee's selfish desires.

My experiences confirm this. I've worked with and

interviewed thousands of managers of hundreds of major brands that rely on teen workers and young professionals. I hear the same story over and over, whether it's about sloppily dressed cashiers at fast food restaurants or new doctors who think (and act as if) patient care ends at 5:00 p.m. on Friday.

The immediate effects of this mentality include a loss of the employer's productivity, higher turnover rates, and slower economic growth. Long-term, it could cause the business to go under. When he leaves the company, Mr. I.M. Special eventually heads off to his next job—or prolonged unemployment—still woefully unprepared to build a career or succeed in life.

Collateral Damage

The ideals of work ethic have suffered such blows that Americans are losing sight of its value. In fact, only 26 percent of adults believe it's still possible for just about anyone to work hard and get rich in America, according to a 2010 Rasmussen poll. That same poll found that 58 percent of adults don't think work ethic will pay off, and another 16 percent weren't sure. And the report showed that adults eighteen to twenty-nine were by far the most pessimistic age group on the topic of work ethic. Work ethic, indeed, is often mentioned by young self-described thought leaders as a major obstacle in achieving work-life balance, as if "work ethic" and "workaholism" were synonymous.

Correcting these misguided notions and instilling a traditional work ethic into the emerging workforce can produce a seismic economic and cultural shift in America. We have great and ever-improving technologies. We have an emerging workforce that embraces change, is better educated and more innovation-focused than any previous generation, and wants to change the world for the better.

All of those advantages, however, can become seeds lost among the weeds. To make sure they find fertile soil, take root, grow, and bear fruit, members of the emerging workforce must shed their notions about being entitled to a job, and about reward coming before effort. In the process, they'll experience a feeling that cannot be bought at any price: the pride of accomplishment, a reward in and of itself.

CHAPTER 2

Coming to Terms with This Thing Called Work Ethic

Remember the old adage that if you find a career you love you'll never work a day in your life? Not true. Every job, no matter how much you love it, involves components that require sacrifice and exertion. That's why it feels good when work ends—there's a sense of accomplishment and pride, and along with it, an expectation of rest, relaxation, and a reward of some kind.

Our view of work has changed so much over the years that we sometimes lose sight of what hasn't changed. Today, our work isn't always measured by the amount of time we spend in the office or how much we perspire— but those are still factors. We still must roll up our sleeves and put in the time to get the work done. And that often involves doing things that lack glamour, that require sacrifice, or that simply aren't easy.

If you ask ten different people to define work ethic, you'll likely get ten different answers. Some might indicate that it's best measured by time, like "putting in long hours," "burning the midnight oil," "pulling a double," or "working around the clock." Others might use a standard of energy exerted: they might say they did "backbreaking labor" or were "spent" after a long day. But before we move forward, we need to come to a consensus.

> "Work is the only thing that gives substance to life."
> —Albert Einstein to his son, Hans, in 1937

For members of the emerging workforce, *work* often looks like something their parents spend too much time focusing on, or something they'll get around to when it's convenient or when they want to buy something in the unlikely event that their parents won't get it for them. And *ethic* may look like something best defined by each individual, not something one person should ever impose on another.

But this ambivalence toward the concept of work ethic raises an interesting question: as long as they demonstrate a good one, does it really matter if your employees know what work ethic is? Probably not. But to lead them and to help them develop one, again, we'll need to agree on a usable definition. As I set out on my quest to clarify what work ethic means in the modern American economy, I began by talking to those who complain about its disappearance the most.

Over the past ten years, I've interacted with, listened to, and surveyed more than 1,500 employers (business owners, C-level executives, HR professionals, managers, supervisors, etc.) in an attempt to understand what work ethic looks like from their perspective. In each exchange,

I listened to their various laments about that lack of work ethic and responded by asking this question:

"What do you expect from each and every employee?"

At the risk of sounding simplistic, I can summarize hundreds of responses in one sentence:

Employers are searching for positive, enthusiastic people who show up for work on time, who are dressed and prepared properly, who go out of their way to add value and do more than what's required of them, who are honest, who will play by the rules, and who will give cheerful, friendly service regardless of the situation.

Consider for a moment the seven elements that comprise that sentence. Together, they sum up what you want from your people, don't they? Regardless of your current employment situation—even if you're fully staffed—I'll bet my house that you'd always find a way to hire someone who was

- upbeat, optimistic, energetic, and positive
- dependable, no matter what
- neatly groomed, appropriately dressed, and well mannered
- ambitious and dedicated (not satisfied with merely "good enough")
- trustworthy (uncompromisingly honest)
- coachable (i.e., recognized your authority and conformed to your rules and company policies)

- determined to do anything necessary to delight every customer and coworker

Right now, you're probably thinking of one or two very special individuals who work (or worked) for you. "Wow. You've just described _____." The name you put in that blank belongs to someone who consistently demonstrates each and every one of those seven core values, doesn't it? Had that person been deficient in any of those areas, his or her name wouldn't have popped into your mind.

While you're thinking of that very special employee, imagine that an admissions rep for a graduate program at a prestigious university called to get a reference and asked you about the employee's work ethic. Would your description be anything less than stellar?

Unless I'm way off the mark, we're in alignment on this. Those seven elements are essential when addressing an individual's work ethic. The list is both comprehensive and complete, and it doesn't mention any specific skill set, time parameters, or specific physical attributes or requirements. That's because the essentials of work ethic are core values, not skills.

I'll be the first to admit that this description is a bit long for a usable definition of work ethic. In an effort to shorten it up, I hit the library.

Most dictionary definitions of work ethic present it as a noun and describe it as a static concept—an ideal or a belief. I think this misses the mark, because real-world work ethic is alive and active, not merely a concept one ponders or aspires to. Fortunately, the term becomes clearer when you look at the words individually.

Webster's defines *ethics* as "the discipline dealing with what is good and bad" and *ethic* as "a theory or system of moral values" or "a guiding philosophy." Essentially, ethics involves *knowing* right from wrong. *Work* is defined by action—the effort sustained to overcome and achieve a result. Therefore, we can say that work ethic is *knowing* the right thing to do, and then *doing* it.

The French term *savoir faire* suggests that a person has the ability to react well in any situation. *Savoir* means to *know*, and *faire* means to *do*. We're on to something here.

So we have our nice, brief definition, but we come to a hiccup when we have to discuss the fact that work ethic is made up of "core values." How can we universally agree on what is meant by a positive value or "the right thing"? We're living in a time when any mention of a person's values is an opening for debate informed by political correctness and moral relativity. The focus is *whatever works for you* as opposed to *whatever works for me*. To find the common ground and fully understand the nature of the values that make up work ethic, let's revisit preadolescence, when we were toddlers in a sandbox.

Sandbox Values

When children are old enough to understand and comprehend basic commands, parents and teachers begin subtly and overtly programming their value systems. This begins shortly after birth and increases daily, all in an attempt to help the little tykes make good choices; their parents and teachers hope these good choices will help them live a happier and more successful life.

The common messages behind the values taught to children transcend cultural, ethnic, gender, religious, and economic differences. Children all around the world are taught to

- Smile and play nice.
- Be prompt.
- Look their best.
- Do their best.
- Obey the rules.
- Tell the truth.
- Say *please* and *thank you*.

Now compare those Sandbox Values to the sentence I used to summarize what I learned when asking business leaders what they are looking for in their employees:

Universal Sandbox Values	Employers Want
Smile and play nice	Positive, enthusiastic people
Be prompt	who show up on time
Look your best	dressed and prepared properly
Do your best	go out of their way to add value/do more than required
Obey the rules	play by the rules
Tell the truth	are honest
Say *please* and *thank you*	give cheerful, friendly service

As you can see, the work ethic that employers desire is rooted in the exact same lessons we all learned as toddlers.

That brings us to an interesting and relevant question. If we teach these values to children, why are employers tearing their hair out looking for young employees who exhibit them?

The answer is that as children grow out of being cute and adorable, they move into adolescence—where everything changes.

Toddlers perform for their parents, but as they mature into their teens, kids begin performing for their peers and imitating the behaviors of their idols and heroes (usually stars in sports, music, or TV and movies). And with reality television taking us ever deeper into the lives of these larger-than-life celebrities, it's painfully obvious that most are not polite, punctual, honest, cheerful people who play by the rules. Most, in fact, exemplify the direct opposite of each of these core values. Yet, they have the cool toys, the fame, and the glory.

No wonder teens and young adults look at the Sandbox Values and either question them, ignore them, or completely rewrite them to fit their worldview. As young people wrestle with differences between the values they were taught and the values they see on display around them, they experience *cognitive dissonance*, which Wikipedia defines as "an uncomfortable feeling caused by holding conflicting ideas simultaneously." Psychologists point out that people have a motivational drive to reduce this dissonance by changing their attitudes and beliefs to rationalize and justify their behavior. Unfortunately, it is usually the more immediate influence—peer pressure and celebrity media—that wins out over the values handed down to them by their parents.

While cognitive dissonance and rejecting an elder's values is nothing new, some employers naïvely believe that it's not worth spending much time and effort to address. Young people always have failed in their early jobs, they say, and they've always been deficient in work ethic. They aren't "there," these folks argue, because they are just like every other generation of kids who weren't "there" at this stage of life. Leave them alone, they say, and these kids will figure it out on their own.

It's true that every generation struggles to some degree with learning work ethic. But a lack of work ethic has become a systemic, defining quality in our culture—not just a brief phase of life for some teenagers. The attitudes and practices that destroy work ethic often are taught, encouraged, and promoted. And the adults who don't see the problem often lack the values they think the younger generations will magically acquire. The "kids will be kids" defense is nothing more than a lame excuse for doing nothing at a time when it's never been more important to act. Our work ethic pandemic won't right itself if we look the other way, and addressing it starts with the emerging workforce because of its size and its opportunity for long-term impact.

Seven Simple But Powerful Terms

To bridge the gap between the Sandbox Values and the values that make up work ethic, I've listed seven terms—markers, if you will—that summarize the values that are common to both. Each is a familiar workplace term, and each serves as a chapter in this book—a component that allows us to delve into ways leaders can develop these values within their people.

Employers Want	Work Ethic Markers
Positive, enthusiastic people	Positive Attitude
who show up on time	Reliability
dressed and prepared properly	Professionalism
go out of their way to add value/do more than required	Initiative
play by the rules	Respect
are honest	Integrity
give cheerful, friendly service	Gratitude

There are no negotiables in this list. By that I mean that there isn't any one of the work ethic markers to which you, as a leader, don't personally aspire and hold yourself accountable. Likewise, you expect these same core values to be evident in everyone you work for, work with, and oversee.

But before we launch into a strategic discussion of how we can develop each of them—and perhaps even more elementary that than, why the challenge of developing these core values in the emerging workforce now rests with employers—let's bring this full circle and take a look at our new definition of work ethic:

Work ethic is knowing what to do and doing it. It

is marked by an individual's positive attitude, reliability, professionalism, initiative, respect, integrity, and gratitude.

Instilling those seven attributes into the hearts and minds of the emerging workforce is the key to keeping our companies, and our country, stable and prosperous. For America's young employees, work ethic is the key to success, whether they are flipping burgers, roofing houses, checking a patient's blood pressure, or piloting spacecraft for NASA.

So when I say most young workers aren't "there" when it comes to work ethic, I can assure you it's a reality worth fighting to change. Your success and the success of your business depend on it.

■ ■ ■

CHAPTER 3

Up and Over— The Leader's Challenge

When an employee reports for his first day on the job, there are some general assumptions and expectations on both sides of the employment equation. The most basic among these is that the employer expects the employee to perform certain tasks, and the employee expects to be compensated for his performance.

However, in addition to the basic money-for-performance expectation, the employer also assumes that the employee understands and will abide by the universal Sandbox Values. If all employees followed these rules, this book would not exist, and neither would 90 percent of employee-related challenges.

In the simplest of terms, employers expect employees to remember the values they learned as kids—whenever and wherever they learned them—and adhere to them in the workplace. The following chart makes a direct correlation between those universal values taught during childhood and those comprising the underpinnings of a solid work ethic necessary for success in any job, in any organization, in any industry.

Universal Sandbox Values	Work Ethic Markers
Smile and play nice	Positive Attitude
Be prompt	Reliability
Look your best	Professionalism
Do your best	Initiative
Obey the rules	Respect
Tell the truth	Integrity
Say *please* and *thank you*	Gratitude

There are a great number of managers today who are frustrated and angry because their expectation of seeing these seven work ethic markers in their people are not being realized—in part or in full—by the talent in the current labor pool. While it would be easy to point the finger at the youngest members in that pool, this is far from a generational issue.

The fact of the matter is, work ethic has been in decline for decades, and the entitlement mentality has stained workers of all ages in all levels and forms of employment. It is, however, much easier to instill positive core values in younger workers who've not yet allowed bad workplace behaviors to become deeply rooted, thus forming unbreakable habits.

This is not a quick fix.

There is no silver-bullet solution.

And it is a call to leadership that will test the mettle of those who seek to revive work ethic and restore the pride of accomplishing great things in their people and throughout their organizations.

The Work Ethic Matrix

To visually illustrate the process that must take place to instill work ethic, let's begin by revisiting our definition:

Work ethic is knowing what to do and doing it. It is marked by an individual's positive attitude, reliability, professionalism, initiative, respect, integrity, and gratitude.

Let's use a horizontal axis to represent a worker's knowledge or "cognizance" of how those seven markers affect their value to an employer. This is the "knowing what to do" part of the definition. So ignorance—not knowing what to do—resides on the left side of the axis. The more a worker learns about what she should do, the more she moves to the right, toward the "know" side.

Figure 1

We'll then overlay a vertical axis to represent an individual's choices, actions, and behaviors as they relate to the seven work ethic markers. This is their "compliance"—the "doing it" part of the definition. Inactivity—not doing what they should be doing—resides at the bottom. The more they "do"—in other words, the more they demonstrate behavior proving they know the core values of work ethic—the more they move upward.

Figure 2

By dissecting the cognitive axis (*don't know* and *know*) with the compliance axis (*don't do* and *do*), we can begin to see four distinct quadrants of behavior.

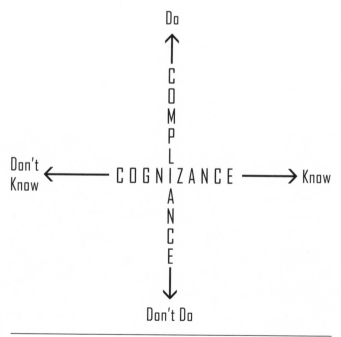

Figure 3

THE IDLE QUADRANT

In the bottom-left quadrant are employees who don't understand work ethic (or any specific marker of it) and don't live it out. Quite simply, they don't know what any of these seven core values really mean or how they play out in the workplace. If they heard these values expressed as a child, they left them behind in the sandbox, or they were stripped of them in their adolescence. As a result, they don't demonstrate the behavior that is expected of them by their employers.

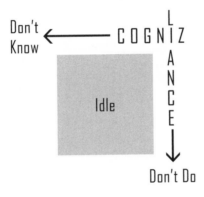

Figure 4

What's confusing is that a worker operating in the Idle Quadrant can possess valuable work skills, but without the work ethic to drive them, he or she is stagnant. Whether ignorant, nonconforming, or just lazy, idle workers are of little or no value to their employers.

THE LUCKY QUADRANT

If you've ever played a game without understanding all the rules and won anyway, you've experienced blind luck. This is similar to a worker who has no real comprehension of the markers of work ethic, but takes action that coincidentally demonstrates a core work ethic value. Although the outcome is positive, the behavior is not fueled by commitment, so it's unsustainable.

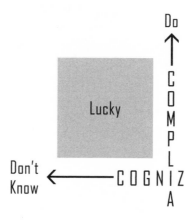

Figure 5

Lucky workers may actually spend much of their time in the Idle Quadrant, but sometimes, without any clear intention, they do something that ends up being a good thing. They show up on time not because they felt a responsibility to show up on time, but because traffic was fast one day. The lucky worker may appear reliable, but it's based on blind luck. The occasional positive results of those in the Lucky Quadrant aren't worth the inevitable decline they will experience without a clearly defined work ethic.

THE CHEATING QUADRANT

She knows she isn't allowed to send text messages while she's on the clock, but while she's waiting on a customer, she texts her boyfriend to resolve a fight. He knows you want him to wear a sport coat and tie to the meeting, but he pretends he didn't get the e-mail and shows up with a mock-neck T-shirt and Dockers.

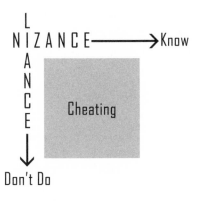

Figure 6

The quadrant in the lower right is where we lose people who understand what they should do but choose not to live it out. This cheating behavior is the most dangerous to leaders, because it pits them squarely at odds with their people. It isn't reserved for "bad people"; we all do things from time to time that are in contrast with our values. To expect that no one will ever cheat to any degree is to demand perfection, and it's unrealistic. But employers want to be able to trust their people to do the right thing whenever a choice between right and wrong presents itself. Unfortunately, because young employees have been so overtly exposed to people who've been able to cheat the system and get away with it, there are more workers residing in the Cheating Quadrant than ever before.

THE VALUED QUADRANT

Workers who possess a clear knowledge of the seven individual markers of core work ethic, and, as a result, make decisions and choices that demonstrate those markers are operating in an optimal state. These are the workers that make up the Valued Quadrant. They are valued both for who they are and what they do, while also providing value to their employers, their customers, and their community.

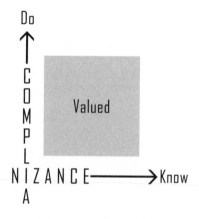

Figure 7

This upper-right quadrant is where you want each and every person in your organization, every person at every level in every job—no exceptions. Those who understand work ethic and intentionally live it out are of the most value to you. They have values, they value themselves, others value them, and they bring value to the organization and the world around them.

So, in an effort to increase the value of their people, the best leaders help them improve both their knowledge (cognizance) of the work ethic markers and the actions (compliance) that demonstrate that knowledge in the workplace.

The idle, the cheating, and the lucky all have one thing in common: they are worthless to their employer. Anyone who stays in those quadrants, even for a brief period of time, is simply *worth less* to themselves and their employers than when they are in the Valued Quadrant. And workers who spend large chunks of time in those other quadrants end up damaging their future and hurting their organization. Whatever good they provide is not worth the risks and costs that come with their behaviors. Improving their understanding of work ethic and motivating them to live out those values is how you move them out of the three lesser quadrants and into a place of value.

The Skills/Work Ethic Paradox

Major sports teams—and their coaches, scouts, owners, and fans—have all experienced the heartbreak of a syndrome best referred to as "the bust.'" A team spends a top draft pick on a highly talented prospect who demonstrates herculean strength—a player who can jump out of the gym, throw a ball a mile, and run like a gazelle. He's uniquely gifted and, with the smell of championships in the air, the team is elated to sign him to a big, expensive contract. But in spite of all his God-given talent, the player never produces anything of value for the team. The prospect is benched and eventually tagged a bust.

And what about the high draft picks in your organization? How many have been busts? They showed up flashing the skills, the academic degrees, the resumes, and the references. They interviewed well and you made the effort to bring them on and put their skills to work for you. But the person who showed up to work was not the one you interviewed. You thought you were bringing on a budding superstar, and you ended up with a bust. But don't point the finger just yet.

The unfortunate reality, in fact, is that all of us experience moments when we ourselves have been busts and moved in and out of the lower quadrants—times when we are "worth less" to ourselves and to our organizations. Ever find yourself sitting at your workstation between tasks, daydreaming about the big game or the date you had the night before? Ever lack the motivation to learn a new skill that would increase your productivity? Ever just get paralyzed by indecision? If so, you've been idle. Ever take on a project where you have no idea what you're doing, but dig in anyway and get lucky? Ever drive faster than the posted speed limit, pay fewer taxes than you owe, or fudge on an expense report to cover a lost receipt? Then you've cheated. You weren't born in the Valued Quadrant, and it's not easy to live there.

That's why it's critically important for leaders to avoid labeling people by the quadrant they occupy at any moment. If, while reading this chapter, you began to associate specific names to quadrants, (i.e., Jeremiah is idle, and Lucy's definitely a cheater) catch yourself before you fall into this dangerous trap. Jeremiah might be idle and Lucy may have cheated, but they can be pulled up and over. You can influence their core values and move them into the Valued Quadrant, but only if you can first see the potential in them. If you label them, they'll sense it, and you will have lost them.

Workers, and not just those in the emerging workforce, move in and out of the four quadrants of work ethic all the time. We all move up and down and from side to side. If we aren't intentionally trying to stay in the Valued Quadrant, we inevitably move out of it.

Great leaders find ways to move people to the right and up on the Work Ethic Matrix and inspire them to operate in a valued state.

Up and over.

Over and up.

How do you move others (and yourself) into the Valued Quadrant?

You do that by reaching into those other quadrants and pulling whoever is there up and to the right. You teach them what they need to know and you motivate and inspire them to do it. It's a role best defined as part teacher and part motivator. It's in this role that a leader distances herself from being a mere manager by adding real value to her people and her organization.

Hey! This Isn't What I Signed Up For!

Who prepared you for your first job? Who instilled the core work ethic that has served as the foundation for your success? With few exceptions, everyone above the age of thirty immediately credits their parents.

For centuries, parents have taken the responsibility for preparing their kids for work. Before I turned in my first job application for a part-time job at Baskin-Robbins, my dad sat me down for a long heart-to-heart chat and told me what I had to do to stand out from other applicants. He told me to go alone, and he told me how to dress, how to fill out the application, and how to sell myself in an interview. When I got the job, after he'd celebrated my personal victory, he put his large hands on my shoulders and sternly said, "If you get fired, don't come home."

I began this chapter by describing the basic expectation an employer has when an employee reports on day one. Though the basic expectations have not changed in the past fifty years, it's both naïve and unrealistic to think that today's parents are taking the same steps that my parents—and yours—took to prepare their kids with the core work ethic that underpins success.

Schools aren't filling the gap, either. We demand that our schools prepare students for college, not for a part-time job. But does college demand the same values they'll need to take to their first hourly dishwashing job—and their first corporate job, and their second? In most cases, the answer is no. Schools are not teaching our kids how to work.

This means the challenge for moving employees up and over to the Valued Quadrant is on you, the employer. You can spend all your time, energy, and resources trying to hire people who already possess a solid work ethic, or you can take actionable steps to create a culture that introduces and develops it. The surest way to win in the new economy is to get really good at hiring the best and developing the work ethic in the rest.

And that is what being an Up and Over Leader is all about.

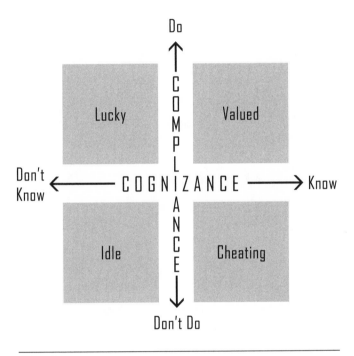

Figure 8

CHAPTER 4

WHAT HAPPENS WHEN YOU'RE NOT WATCHING

Any manager can get people to do what he wants as long as he is standing next to them insisting that they do it. But what happens when the manager turns away? The workers must feel an internal need to comply with what they know is right, without supervision. They have to know what they're supposed to do, and they have to do it without the manager standing over them. Cognizance and compliance— knowing what you should do, and then doing it.

> "Great leaders are almost always great simplifiers, who can cut through argument, debate, and doubt, to offer a solution everybody can understand."
> —Colin Powell

Increasing Employee Cognizance

There are three essential components of developing cognizance in the emerging workforce (and three essential components of ensuring compliance, discussed later in the chapter). I'll share an overview of those with you now, but I'll come back to them frequently in subsequent chapters to show how they play out in specific ways when developing a positive attitude, reliability, professionalism, integrity, respect, initiative, and gratitude.

CLARIFY

If you aren't communicating clearly with your workers, they'll never really understand your expectations, whether it has to do with a hard skill or with values. Of course, most managers and leaders are experts at training the hard skills. *Here's how you clock in. Here's how you clean the deep fryer. Here's how you greet a customer. Here are the forms for tracking time for billing our clients*, and so on.

But it's equally important to provide clarity when it comes to the values of work ethic. And unlike most hard skills, values require regular and significant maintenance. You have to regularly communicate in crystal-clear terms the things workers need to know to live out these values.

Here's how reliability plays out at ACME Corp . . .

Initiative is one of our core values, and it's best demonstrated when a team member does these things . . .

We never want customers to feel unimportant at Burger World, so we don't just smile and say thank you. We infuse our gratitude into each transaction by . . .

You can't teach these things once and expect them to hold forever any more than you can expect to jump from the ground and float in the air. Remember that the young people you are trying to mold are neck-deep in media-hyped stories of celebrities displaying the polar opposite of these values. You must regularly and clearly communicate standards, information, and expectations. A failure to clarify results in a "mind dump" attempt at knowledge transfer, and not much of value grows in a landfill.

ASSESS

Consider what happens on the first day of school for the average fifth-grade student in America. His teacher assumes that all of her students are reporting with a zero-rating in terms of what they need to know for passing the fifth grade, and her goal is to get them to a score of one hundred by the end of the academic year, making them ready to move to grade six.

We don't expect kids to be perfect, however, so we will pass them to the sixth grade if they achieve a rating of seventy or higher. Further, teachers aren't sure what the students actually know and understand and what they just successfully guessed at, but with so many students and so little time, this is close enough, right?

This scenario is based upon flawed logic and provides an argument for an overhaul of our education system. A fifth-grade teacher inherits a class of individuals at various levels, and only a few might actually be at a zero-rating. Some students really didn't comprehend all they should have learned from fourth grade, so they report on the first day at a minus-ten or a minus-twenty. Some are advanced, however, and come in at a plus-eight or even an off-the-charts plus-thirty-three. If she starts teaching as if all the students are at a zero, she'll quickly lose the ones who are at minus-twenty, because they lack the base layers to keep up. What's even worse is that she's going to bore those who are ahead of grade level because they have little interest in relearning what they already know.

What makes it more complicated is that no teacher can correctly judge all the books by their covers. Maybe a student is a mini-Einstein and doesn't look or act like it because he's bored to tears. He could be quiet and withdrawn, or he could be a troublemaker or the class clown. Another student could look or act in the exact same way, not out of boredom, but because she's lost and scared because she thinks she's dumber than her classmates.

This is why good teachers, good managers, good trainers, and good leaders never assume. Instead, they assess. Before they begin imparting knowledge to take their pupils where they need them to go, they first determine where the learner is. Assessment is a crucial step on the path to developing cognizance; you can't help build it unless you know where to start.

To be clear, that's "assess," not "test." Testing can be an effective tool for assessing, especially in education, but it's not the end-all answer. Especially when you're talking about work ethic values, nothing replaces assessment in the form of conversation and dialogue.

Some workers, like some students, won't say anything when they don't really understand what you're telling them. They will act like they got it because they don't want to look stupid. They will fool you into assuming that they are on board and ready to roll—that they know what they need to know—when, in fact, they're heading for a crash.

Other workers are more advanced. In the hope of making a good impression or out of fear of rocking the boat, they keep their mouths shut and politely nod during instruction, all the while concealing the fact that they are bored out of their minds and looking for the escape hatch.

MENTOR

Once you've clarified your goals and expectations with regard to work ethic, and once you've assessed what your worker knows and needs to learn, the next step in developing cognizance is embracing your role as a teacher/coach/trainer and providing the ongoing instruction that builds and establishes an understanding of the things they really need to know.

Developing cognizance through teaching requires a combination of factors. The emerging workforce is used to high-speed presentations with catchy graphics and interactions that create an adrenaline rush, but nothing replaces a one-on-one, heart-and-soul teacher mentality. It's got to be more than a talking head on a video or an online training session. You're going to need a variety of approaches so that you can teach in ways that introduce and reinforce a clear message that addresses the specific needs of each person. And that's why you need to assess before you edify and mentor.

Organizations can use different methods and models for teaching and reteaching the values that drive success, but the ones with no methods or models eventually will have one thing in common: failure.

Increasing Employee Compliance

There are two axes that create the Work Ethic Matrix, and it's not enough to move someone along just one of them. The goal, remember, is to move them up and over, over and up. Developing cognizance without working hard to gain compliance is akin to entering vast amounts of data into a computer and then unplugging it; it is a waste of time and resources. The computer has to operate to create any value from the data. So let's look at three key elements for generating buy-in for work ethic values.

RELEVANCE

Members of the emerging workforce need to know the why before they will take action on the what. "Don't just tell me what to do," they say (or think). "Tell me why I'm doing it." *Because I said so,* once a silver bullet in the arsenals of parents everywhere, now has all the impact of a water pistol.

The "what" is the action you want your workers to take: answering the phone professionally, wearing a hair net while in the kitchen, submitting an expense report each Tuesday. Sometimes we attach an ultimatum to the "what" in an effort to coerce employees into the desired behavior: "We prosecute all employee theft." "If you're more than ten minutes late, you may be sent home." "Raises are only given to those who memorize the company values."

For some employees, getting the "what" as a command is sufficient. These workers are simply wired to do as they are told, or they live in fear of negative consequences. But for others—and the percentage that falls into this category is growing faster than the national debt—the only way to achieve consistent compliance on any desired outcome is to provide the rationale; the *why* behind the *what.*

Explaining the relevance of the desired action is a way of connecting the dots between *what* and *why*. Making the relevance clear requires stating the obvious, but then going well beyond it. You might say, "We need you to show up on time at 6:30 a.m. because we open at 7:00 a.m., and you will need thirty minutes to set up everything and make a killer impression on our customers when they walk in the door. Our reputation for opening on time is essential for gaining a loyal and growing customer base."

Now you've told your employee what he needs to know and why it's relevant—to you. Sometimes that's enough, but most of the time it's not. The next step is to help him understand why arriving thirty minutes before the store opens is relevant to him, because the question racing through his mind is this: "If we open at 7:05 or 7:20, I still get $8.50 an hour, right?"

Effective relevance comes full circle. So in this scenario, you might make the desired *what* (showing up at 6:30) relevant to him by adding, "And naturally, the more loyal returning customers we have, the more money we have in the till for raises."

You also could seal the relevance by helping your young hire understand the connection between punctual openings, loyal customers, and opportunities for advancement. Or you might counter his tendency to grow bored by letting him know that increased customer traffic makes time go by much quicker. Finally, you could appeal to his sense of adventure by telling him that a busy store increases the odds that he'll get to meet interesting people.

By their very nature, young people are inwardly

focused and tend to see life only as it relates to their own world. If they are late or rude or slow or negative and they have a reason to justify it, they think you should cut them some slack. After all, they do what they are supposed to most of the time, and any fallout can be fixed, right?

That's ridiculous, of course. However, you need to understand the "me bubble" that most young employees are immersed in. Once you do, you can take steps to help them look beyond themselves to see how their attitudes, decisions, behaviors, and actions at work affect more than just themselves.

Effective leaders frequently find themselves luring workers out of their "me bubble" by showing them how their choices affect others—their bosses, their coworkers, their company, their customers, and their community. Young people want to be of value; they often just need a mentor to show them the bigger picture—how what their doing is relevant to the world around them.

Threats of dire consequences are not nearly as effective as they once were, because today's youth don't scare easily. It is far easier to penetrate their bubble and achieve compliance to your standards by providing an "I win, you win, the company wins, the customer wins, and the world is a better place in the process" connection.

REWARD

If you work with, manage, or otherwise deal regularly with members of the emerging workforce, chances are you know what to do when you catch someone who breaks the rules. You have a policy and a plan for dealing with the chronically late employee, the individual who has taken personal liberties with the required uniform, or the cashier who is caught taking money from the register. Your eyes are peeled. You have the lecture memorized. The consequences are written in stone tablets, and you have HR on speed dial.

So what do you do for the worker who has never lied to you or hasn't missed a day of work in over a year? What about the person who always arrives with a clean, pressed apron and fully covers her tattoos as laid out in the company handbook? What kind of recognition is given to the average performer who meets, but doesn't exceed, the company's standards?

Most organizational cultures expect this type of behavior and ignore it, focusing instead only on the remarkably good or the remarkably bad. We punish the negative and praise the positive, and we completely ignore anything in the middle. You might ask, "Should I really reward someone for doing what she should do in the first place? Isn't that the wrong message?" There are dangers in over-rewarding what should be standard behavior, and I've already noted the world's tendency to reward non-behavior or even

> "Appreciate everything your associates do for the business. Nothing else can quite substitute for a few well-chosen, well-timed, sincere words of praise. They're absolutely free and worth a fortune."
> —Sam Walton

poor behavior. But there are ways to build in incentives and rewards that encourage and reinforce positive behaviors and create habits that become the building blocks for excellence.

These rewards can be extremely creative or as simple as a well-timed word of praise. The good habits formed on the trail of rewards end up creating values that are a reward in and of themselves. That's because practicing the values that make up work ethic isn't a punishment; it produces rewards. But those rewards can be hard to see until you're living out the values. It's a catch-22, so at times they need a little booster shot to get going.

I've been invited to speak on the campuses of more than 1,500 high schools throughout North America, and every one has an attendance policy, as well as a policy defining acceptable conduct, behavior, and academic performance. Each school clearly communicates with students and their parents and explains the consequences that are imposed for those who do not comply.

However, the schools where I've experienced the best cultures, and the schools that boast the greatest performance records, are the ones that find ways to celebrate compliance. They do more than conduct pep rallies for the star athletes and celebrate top achievements of their scholars; they provide rewards for all students who meet ambitious—but achievable—standards in academics, attendance, and character. In these special environments, everyone clearly understands what is expected of them, and those who demonstrate compliance are rewarded with special activities, events, and benefits reserved for rule followers.

Business leaders can take a valuable lesson from this and create a reward structure that promotes a positive work ethic, not just incentives for those who achieve above-and-beyond excellence. We'll touch on ways to do this as we move into subsequent chapters.

RADIATE

The most powerful values of an organization are radiated throughout the culture. Disney World, for example, celebrates the professional appearance of its employees, so it's abnormal to see anyone not following the dress code to the letter. And Wegmans, the family-owned supermarket chain in the Northeast, rewards employees for taking initiative and finding ways to add value for their stores during slow periods. These companies infuse core work ethic values into their cultures. By celebrating the people who demonstrate these values, the values radiate throughout the organizations.

Several years ago I spoke to an all-school assembly at Oshkosh North High School in Wisconsin, and I was impressed by how the school's leaders radiated a vision for achievement by hanging inspiring portraits in the hallways. Unlike other schools I had visited, the portraits displayed at ONHS weren't of presidents or famous athletes or wealthy donors. Instead, these were portraits of graduates from the high school who had accomplished significant things in their careers and now were leading productive, successful lives in their communities.

Radiate, a transitive verb, means to spread something all around as it emanates from a center. The key to radiating values is to establish them as central ideals and then find ways to spread them throughout teams and organizations. That includes living them out yourself, of course, but it also includes celebrating them, hiring people who display them, incorporating them in company meetings and communications, and sharing them with those who need them the most.

Leaders radiate core values when they cite them during performance evaluations or, better yet, when performance evaluations are centered around the values. Rather than allowing the values to fade into a forgotten mission statement, leaders can use the words frequently in company meetings and provide public praise for employees who demonstrate them in exceptional ways.

The concept of radiating values defies the myth that work ethic demands isolation. For months I tracked Internet stories about "work ethic," and almost all of the articles were about athletes—a coach was praising an athlete's work ethic. The second big category was when someone was retiring or receiving an award for a job well done. The third category was self-praise, which usually involved a politician promising to demonstrate great work ethic. The term was always applied to a single person—never to a team, company, or association.

It can become easy to see work ethic as something individuals do, even to the point of the negative—*her work ethic keeps her isolated and driven to self-achievement.* Many people conjure up images of a person staying late, alone at the office, when they hear the phrase. That's why you must radiate these values throughout the culture and harness the full potential of creating teams that promote and live out work ethic. Real work ethic always thrives best in community, not in isolation.

We now have a working definition of work ethic: knowing what to do and doing it, as marked by positive attitude, reliability, professionalism, initiative, respect, integrity, and gratitude.

And we have a visual model for what's needed to instill the values of work ethic by increasing cognizance (knowing) and compliance (doing) to move workers up and over, over and up, so that they end up in the Valued Quadrant—as employees who are valued for who they are and what they bring to the organization.

And we know that clarity, assessment, and mentoring are keys to increasing cognizance, while relevance, rewards, and radiation drive compliance.

Now it's time to dive more deeply into the qualities that you'll see in someone who really lives out work ethic at its best. In the next seven chapters, we'll talk about what those values are, what they aren't, why they are important to work ethic, and, most important, how to instill them in the emerging workforce.

Universal Sandbox Values	Employers Want	Work Ethic Markers
Play nice, smile, and be polite	Positive, enthusiastic people	Positive Attitude
Be prompt	who show up on time	Reliability
Look your best	dressed and prepared properly	Professionalism
Do your best	go out of their way to add value/do more than required	Initiative
Obey the rules	play by the rules	Respect
Tell the truth	are honest	Integrity
Say *please* and *thank you*	give cheerful, friendly service	Gratitude

CHAPTER 5

POSITIVE ATTITUDE

"Nothing can stop the man with the right mental attitude from achieving his goal; nothing on earth can help the man with the wrong mental attitude."
—*Thomas Jefferson*

It's hard to imagine a more enjoyable summer job for a student than working at a large, ultramodern amusement park filled with a variety of games and attractions, all sorts of guilty-pleasure foods, and dozens of thrilling rides. Seems like the last place on earth you'd find stone-faced, bored-to-tears young employees, especially when those employees are well paid and pampered with perks.

Yet, there I was back in 1995, walking through the largest and most celebrated theme park in the Rocky Mountain region with a photo nametag clipped to my shirt that identified me as "Eric: The Attitude Guy." My job? To make the teen workers throughout Denver's Elitch Gardens theme park happy, and to remind them to smile and have fun so that the patrons would sense and share in the happiness.

In other words, I was hired to peddle a positive attitude to employees.

The senior leadership at Elitch Gardens had grown tired of the dismal feedback on guest surveys, most relating to the disengaged service and lack of attention from the frontline staff. I had given a presentation at one of Elitch's leadership retreats, and the management was familiar with my work as a motivational speaker and author who worked with teens, so they thought I might help turn things around by doing some one-on-one work with their young workers.

It sounded like a dream job. They allowed me the freedom to come and go as I wanted and paid me an extremely generous consulting fee to simply stroll through the park and spread good cheer to 1,500 young workers who were hawking snow cones, giving away stuffed animals in the arcades, and loading patrons onto the roller coasters. They provided an endless stream of incentives (logo apparel, concert tickets, park merchandise, etc.) that I could dole out as I deemed necessary to achieve the desired result: smiling, happy crew members.

But the dream job wasn't so dreamy. Frankly, it was one of the worst assignments I ever accepted. As much as I enjoy speaking to groups of kids or working with them when we can form a relationship, I'm not Zippo the Clown. And even when I could turn a kid's frown upside down, it was just a quick fix, not a solution to the overarching problem.

Organizations all across the country have battled attitude problems for decades, and not just in industries that require backbreaking hard labor. And nowhere is the attitude of the organization in more full view of the customer than along the organization's frontline; the precious eighteen inches of attitude that are projected between the nose of the employee and the nose of the customer.

Young workers haven't always been synonymous with bad attitude; in fact, they were once noted for being inherently happy. They hadn't been soured by the doldrums and monotony of the forty-hour, nose-to-the-grindstone workweek, and they were fresh, eager, and ready to please. Employers hired teenagers with an expectation that they were trading experience for youthful exuberance. But those days are gone.

There now exists a pandemic of young people who are disillusioned, disenfranchised, disengaged, and depressed, and who carry those attitudes with them into the workplace. Don't take my word for it. Go observe the transactions between customers and frontline service employees at your local mall, theater, or nearby amusement park. Unless you reside in Pleasantville or are watching workers who rely on tips for their daily bread, I predict you won't see many happy, smiling, young faces.

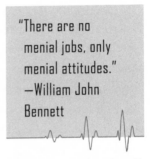

"There are no menial jobs, only menial attitudes."
—William John Bennett

The Power of Positive

Attitude is nothing more and nothing less than a person's outward expression of his internal views. It is where your perceptions become your realities. So to define your attitude, you need only answer three questions.

How do you see yourself?

How do you see the world?

How do you see yourself in the world?

The first two questions set up the third, and the answer to the third question—how do you see yourself in the world?—is the determining factor of your attitude.

Conveniently, the answers to all three questions are totally within your control. You get to choose how you see yourself, how you see the world, and how you see yourself in the world—no matter how others see you, how the world sees you, or how others see you in the world. You get to pick the glasses you'll wear each day as you view yourself and the world around you. You get to decide whether you like the person you are, whether you like your surroundings, whether you like your parents, whether you like your kids, whether you like your boss, whether you like your employees, whether you like the weather . . . It's all your choice, and it all reflects your attitude.

There's nothing groundbreaking in this message. You've probably heard it before, or at least something similar. Henry David Thoreau called thought the "sculptor who can create the person you want to be." And before William James said, "As you think, so shall you be," he read a copy of *As a Man Thinketh* (1902) by James Allen, who wrote, "As you dream, so shall you become." Allen, a pioneer when it comes to promoting the power of positive thinking, put it pretty simply in a different section of his book: "Good thoughts bear good fruit, bad thoughts bad fruit." And Allen founded his ideas about positive thinking on the centuries-old writings of Proverbs 23:7: "For as he thinketh in his heart, so is he" (King James Version).

You no doubt know the importance a positive attitude plays in your ability to bring positive results (success) into your job, career, and life. And in spite of the negative attitudes you see every day, it's not a concept that's somehow been hidden from the emerging workforce. I'd challenge you, in fact, to find a kid over the age of eight who hasn't been lectured to death about the importance of a positive attitude. They get it from their parents, from their teachers, from their coaches, from the clergy, from their scout leaders, and yes, from their employers. The reminders are everywhere they turn.

Why then, are so many teens and young adults on so many prescription drugs to deal with anxiety and depression? How come brand names like Prozac and Zoloft are as well known to them as brands like McDonald's and Nike? Why did a 2010 study by the National Institute of Mental Health (NIMH) find that nearly 50 percent of U.S. teens ages thirteen to eighteen have met the "diagnostic criteria for at least one [mental] disorder over a lifetime" and that 20 percent have suffered from a "mental disorder with symptoms severe enough to impair their daily lives"?

Let's look at four explanations.

1. Negative Is Hip

From where your young employees sit, it's just not cool to be positive. From James Dean to Fonzie and from Pink to Puck, the hippest youth icons generally sport a giant chip on their shoulders and are always looking for a fight. But where you once had to go to the drive-in or wait for your favorite show to come on to see the popular bad boys and girls, today they're hitting you from all sides. Hundreds, if not thousands, of examples of bad attitudes invade the consciousness of today's youth, and the worst offenders usually get the most attention and the biggest contracts.

Smiling, happy teens are viewed by their peers as goofy, spoiled, naïve kiss-ups. But if you're dismissive, have an edge, or create havoc everywhere you go, you're respected and in good company. Trendy teen fashion stores such as Hollister, Aéropostale, Guess, and Abercrombie & Fitch employ—almost exclusively—the young, elite, cool kids in their communities who resemble their pretty-people alter egos in the companies' catalogues. If you study them in malls, you'll see these pouty-faced young employees stare off into space as if they have something much more important and interesting to do than sell the clothing that's funding their paychecks.

2. Work Sucks

From the perspective of the young person, work is a bad thing. You're supposed to hate work; everybody does. Why should young people be happy at work when work is the very thing the authority figures around them (parents, teachers, bosses) constantly complain about? How many times can they hear things, like "I hate my job," "Thank God it's Friday!" "I'm calling in sick," and "As soon as I can find something better, I'm outta here!" without it completely eroding their view of work?

Young people have been raised on the promise that they can have it all and that they don't have to wait until they are old to get it. So if that's true, they reason, why is someone asking them to do the same meaningless task today that they performed yesterday? How can they expect to show up with a happy face when they'd much rather be in the garage jamming with their band or hanging out with friends at the mall? After all, work is a necessary evil, right? It's not supposed to be fun. You hurry up and get it over with—you just want the coin for the pleasures you seek. So why be happy about work?

3. "I was born too late."

Members of the emerging workforce see a world that's filled with the negative. They can't escape the ranting political activists, the news of terrorism and natural disasters, the broken families all around them, and the corporate scandals that leave pension funds empty and executives with golden parachutes.

Today's youth are much more aware of the world around them than any previous generation. The greatest challenge facing the youth of today, in fact, is that they're aware of all the other challenges. A couple of centuries ago, most people were only aware of their own misery, and that was plenty. It took weeks or months to learn about the miseries of people elsewhere around the country, and only the elite knew much about the world's discomforts. Now it comes tweeted instantly with links to live video feeds and constant analysis from a dizzying array of pundits.

Consider all the negativity they are exposed to, and realize they compare it to the repetitive tales they've heard from adults about how great everything was "back in the day" when life was so much simpler, safer, and happier. Ever arrive to a terrific party just as it's breaking up—people leaving, all the food and drinks gone?

Make no mistake: it's hard to stay positive in a negative world.

4. "This isn't what I was promised."

The biggest reason for the growing negativity among young employees, however, is the huge gap between their expectations (what they believe life, work, and school should be like for them) and their reality. They've been told from the time they were knee-high that they were *special, gifted, talented,* and *one-of-a-kind,* and their jobs are sold to them by the interviewer as "a fun place to work." Once they get past the training period, they discover that work is not always easy or glamorous, and seldom is it fun—at least in the way they've come to define the term. They feel jilted. If it's not the job they feel they were promised or are entitled to, they think they must be in the wrong job or working for a boss who doesn't appreciate them.

I did some consulting with a national banking institution, and one of its leaders told me a story about a new young worker's discontent after the first few days on the job. "Is this all there is?" the girl asked. "Is this what I do every day? I come here and do this job, the same thing over and over? This is now my life?"

Coming from a school environment in which there were new classes every nine weeks, lots of extracurricular activities to choose from, and plenty of vacation breaks and assorted days off, she wasn't prepared for the regularity of work. Her new reality was a job that involved repetition, longer hours, and far fewer breaks, and it would be months (or years) before she'd be promoted or given a different assignment. She already had become disenchanted and was experiencing the onset of a massive negative attitude that would be evident to everyone around her.

When expectations aren't met, anger sets in. If I expect the driver next to me to stay in his lane and he doesn't, I tend to get annoyed. If I honk at him expecting him to take the clue and move over and he doesn't, I get more agitated. If I mouth the words, "Get in your own lane!" and instead of mouthing back "I'm sorry" he flips me off, I might feel rage coming on. Anger, in most cases, results from unfulfilled expectations. The same goes for unfulfilled expectations at work, except that some workers channel their anger into more passive, disengaged behaviors.

Leaders Need to Stand Tall (and Smile)

Negative attitudes are like a virus that can be transmitted between young employees and their supervisors. If I expect my employee to be happy because she's getting $9 an hour (when I was her age, I was paid only $1.25 an hour for doing the exact same work!), but she acts entitled to what she's earning and is hinting at wanting even more, that will really piss me off! To make matters worse, she wants to text her friends on company time, but I won't allow it. So I'm angry and she's angry, and her anger makes me even more angry . . . and so on.

As parents, educators, and workforce leaders, our challenge is to inoculate ourselves from the negativity of the younger generation and, instead, help young people embrace a positive attitude. This is not done by telling them the joke of the day or forcing a smile in their direction, but rather by taking sustainable measures to breed positivity into your interactions.

Maintaining a positive, optimistic, enthusiastic attitude—regardless of the situation—is an essential component of every job description. That's why it's always the first thing mentioned when employers are asked what they are looking for in their new hires. Without question, moving the emerging workforce up, over, and into the Valued Quadrant begins with this foundational value.

If you want someone to display a positive attitude at work, you first need to make sure they know what you mean by a positive attitude and what it looks like in your organization. They need to see living examples of positive attitude in action when working for you, and they should be put into situations that allow them to shadow people who model the attitude you are trying to replicate in them. Attitude is contagious, so let them catch the right virus, and go out of your way to make certain they aren't infected with the wrong ones.

Clarifying what a good attitude is begins with the hiring process. You need to be very direct about the duties involved in the job—the good, the bad, and the ugly—so you can get the properly shaped pegs in the properly shaped holes.

I wasn't suited to be The Attitude Guy and had no real idea of what was expected of me, so the reality of the job adversely affected my attitude. In contrast, my son grew up with a friend, Nathan, who had a job in a local theater. As part of his job, Nathan took a cart full of snacks and drinks into the theater before each show started and enthusiastically hawked the stuff to movie-goers. He was a drama student and an aspiring actor who wanted nothing more than to be in front of people. His manager told him that he'd get an opportunity to stand in front of an audience five or ten times each night. Selling to the crowd fit Nathan's personality and his attitude to a tee, and the job fit the description Nathan had been promised by his manager.

Once you're clear on the attitude an employee needs for a specific job, it's important to create a checklist of must-have attitude attributes. You can then use that list to assess a person's attitude. But don't assume anything based on an initial interview; first impressions can be misleading. Everyone puts on a happy face to land the job offer, so go a few layers deeper. Contact references and ask how your young candidate carries himself outside of work. Teachers, coaches, and activity sponsors can turn the lights on for you. Asking open-ended questions in a follow-up interview will help you accurately assess how the candidate responds to stress, strangers, and criticism.

After you make a decision to add anyone to your payroll, it's important to provide frequent evaluations that include feedback about their workplace attitudes. But don't just limit the feedback they get to what *you* think of them; include feedback that comes from their coworkers. Blind 360-degree feedback (where the other evaluators' identities are concealed) helps remove the "me versus you" dynamic from an attitude assessment by allowing them to see themselves through varying perspectives. (Young people love this; that's why their Facebook wall is so important to them.) Learning what others think of their approach to work can be eye opening and serve as the catalyst for a significant attitude adjustment.

Finding Meaning in Attitude

Viktor Frankl's classic book *Man's Search for Meaning* (1946) tells of his experiences as an inmate in a concentration camp during World War II. Amid all the horrors of those experiences, Frankl learned how having a positive attitude can literally save your life.

"We who lived in concentration camps can remember the men who walked through the huts comforting others, giving away their last piece of bread," Frankl wrote. "They may have been few in number, but they offer sufficient proof that everything can be taken from a man but one thing: the last of the human freedoms—to choose one's attitude in any given set of circumstances, to choose one's own way."

Frankl witnessed the power of embracing attitude as a personal choice and taking personal responsibility for the way you view yourself, the world, and yourself in the world—even in a concentration camp.

He wrote, "We can discover this meaning in life in three different ways: (1) by creating a work or doing a deed; (2) by experiencing something or encountering someone; and (3) by the attitude we take toward unavoidable suffering."

Reading or discussing Frankl's masterpiece with younger workers often leads them to conclude that whether they're working a cash register, dealing with unruly patients or customers, cleaning the company bathroom, or performing any other job they think may be beneath them, it all pales in comparison to the sufferings others have unfairly endured. The perspective they get from a story like this, or from many others like it, can have a life-altering impact on the attitude.

Praising the Positive

You'll be hard pressed to find any young individual who hasn't been called out by an adult at some point in her life, and likely multiple times, for having a bad attitude. But few, if any, have been praised or rewarded solely because they have a positive attitude. That means they know what having a bad attitude is, but they may have difficulty accurately defining a positive one. That gives you an opportunity to catch them being positive—and calling it to their attention—with praise or a reward. Remember, what gets rewarded gets repeated.

Be on the lookout for those glimpses of the attitude you're trying to instill in your people, and be prepared to call attention to it. Perhaps you say, "Thanks for being so willing to pull a double, Jake. I knew you had a date and could have put up a stink about working late, but you accepted my request without any hesitation and even smiled, then shifted into high gear and got us out of here at a respectable hour. Thanks, man. Your positive attitude is an example for the others, and I'll make sure the folks at corporate hear about this."

The sooner you acknowledge a positive attitude, the better. A friend's daughter works as a receptionist in a busy clinic at a hospital. One day it snowed and she was the only one of the three receptionists in her department who showed up. Throughout the hospital, in fact, very few receptionists or other frontline workers showed up, which made for a long, stressful day for those who did come in. What if the hospital's CEO had spent an hour walking the halls simply thanking those receptionists for being there? On the other hand, what if no one ever gave them a word of thanks for their exemplary behavior that day?

No matter how you reward employees for displaying a positive attitude, before it becomes a permanent part of who they are at work, they need to see positive attitude as a reward in itself. However, as a leader, it's on you to help them also see how it improves their productivity and their value to your organization, how it endears them to coworkers and customers, and especially how it makes their work more enjoyable.

An Infectious Culture

A positive attitude at work is infectious, so the more you call it out to others and encourage it in key employees, the easier it will be for you to radiate it throughout your culture. This starts with the small things you do, like calling out the guy who works the double or the receptionist who comes in when it's snowing, but it continues with how far you radiate those kinds of things each day.

To create a positive culture, talk to your young people about the good things that are happening throughout your business. If you can't share positive news about the company, shine the light on something good that's taking place in your community, the nation, or the world. Make it your mission to be a purveyor of good tidings. Go out of your way to be the beacon of light when everything else they may be exposed to drags them down.

The manager of a large supermarket in St. Louis told me that she schedules an all-store meeting once each quarter solely to share success stories of employees—both work-related and non-work-related—with her entire team. Although the meetings are not mandatory and begin at 7:00 a.m. on Saturdays, she said the attendance at these meetings is always at or near 100 percent because all the dialogue is centered around the positive things her people are doing.

Many organizations put tons of effort into promoting the good news about their company to the outside world in an effort to attract and keep investors. But they neglect their internal customers—their workers. I've seen customers try to strike up conversations with cashiers about a piece of news they read about the industry or even the specific company the cashier works for, only to have the cashier give them a deer-in-the-headlights look. Take it upon yourself to make your frontline staff feel like an important cog in the wheel of your operation by keeping them informed. Even if you're giving these employees a piece of not-so-good news, they'll be more positive because they feel important.

Make it your mission to help your young employees see that they are on a train that's going somewhere important, and that they are part of something positive and good. Don't stretch small victories into giant ones, but when good things happen, spend as much time telling your frontline workers as you do telling your potential investors. Sure, you want to promote your brand to the world. But don't leapfrog over your frontline employees. Outside investors look in the eyes of your employees every day and decide whether it's a good company—a place they want to invest their money.

Removing the Negative

One of the most effective ways to radiate a positive attitude throughout your culture is to simply look for, and then remove, the things that create a negative attitude. Enter your workplace through the backdoor and see your operation from your employees' perspectives. Is your signage positive, or does it read like it was sent down from the principal's office? There's a big difference between a sign on the employee entrance that says, "All Employees Must Park in the Back Lot" and one that says, "Our Customers Pay Our Wages, So Let's Save the Closest Parking for Them." Carefully edit the negative language and overtones out of employee e-mail, notices, and other forms of communication, and look for creative ways to present them in a more positive way.

Take steps to remove the drab and dreary signs, colors, and broken items that have a way of infesting back areas of workplaces. Managers often allow this to happen because "employees are the only ones exposed to it." You can't isolate your staff members from all the negativity that surrounds them, but you can take steps to remove some of the nastiness from your workplace.

Keep in mind that great employees are out there, but some first impressions can lead you to believe otherwise.

They don't need Zippo the Clown to give them a quick attitude fix. They need a leader who is determined to pull them up into the Valued Quadrant and do whatever it takes to keep them there.

ADDITIONAL CONVERSATION STARTERS AND TIPS FOR INSTILLING A POSITIVE ATTITUDE

In an effort to win control over their own media choices, teens tell their parents that the music they listen to, the games they play, and the television and movies they watch have no impact on how they see the world or the choices they make.

"I can listen to a rapper sing about the injustice of the police and how people need to rise up and take arms and still be a nice, mellow person," they'll say. "I can play *World of Warcraft* or *Halo 3* and never feel a need to be violent. I can watch a raunchy movie and still have the utmost respect for the opposite sex." And with Hollywood's anti-censorship messaging in full force, how can you convince them otherwise? This argument has plagued parents for generations. My dear mother thought "Bad Moon Rising" by Creedence Clearwater Revival came straight from Satan himself.

There isn't a magic age when what we hear and see stops having any kind of influence on us. If the messages we consume on a daily basis were proven to have no impact on our attitudes and behavior, advertising would cease to exist.

The reality is that we're all impressionable.

So, when trying to influence young people whom you believe are ingesting a steady diet of negativity from music, movies, games, and the Internet, don't tell them how media will make them feel or act. Instead, *ask* them how it makes them feel. You can ask them about the media they consume and the people they hang around with. As a leader, it is up to you to determine which questions are appropriate in which settings. Some may gel with your culture while others may not.

- What music would you listen to before you _____ (mention a sport or activity they are involved in)?
- What music/movie/show would get you psyched up for an important game?
- What song would you listen to
  - before taking the SAT?
  - right after your girlfriend breaks up with you?
  - when you're out on a date with someone special?
- What movie would you watch before and after a competition?
- What movie would you take a date to?
- What people would you want to have a conversation with before you
  - take an important test?
  - go on a job interview?
  - go into battle in the state championship wrestling match?

- What friends would you want around
  - before a big date?
  - after a fight with your parents or a coworker?
  - before you go meet with your boss about a promotion or a raise?
- When you approach a challenge or opportunity, what two or three songs, movies, games, or people would be on your playlist?

When they admit to themselves that certain music, movies, games, and people make them feel and act a certain way and help them deal with certain situations, you can build on that to establish two important things: one, that such things affect their attitude when they come to work and, two, that they can have an effect, good or bad, on the people around them.

This is a great technique for taking them out of their "me bubble."

This playlist discussion will help an employee do the things that are necessary to show up for work in the right frame of mind and build an awareness that she is affecting the attitude of her coworkers and clients or customers. She will soon realize that her attitude becomes part of the playlist for everyone she encounters throughout the day.

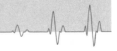

Universal Sandbox Values	Employers Want	Work Ethic Markers
Play nice, smile, and be polite	Positive, enthusiastic people	Positive Attitude
Be prompt	**who show up on time**	**Reliability**
Look your best	dressed and prepared properly	Professionalism
Do your best	go out of their way to add value/do more than required	Initiative
Obey the rules	play by the rules	Respect
Tell the truth	are honest	Integrity
Say *please* and *thank you*	give cheerful, friendly service	Gratitude

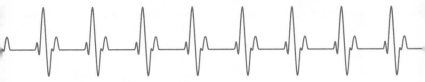

CHAPTER 6

RELIABILITY

*"Capability doesn't have anything to do with reliability.
Some people don't have as much capability as others have, but
they make up for their lack by being reliable."*
—John Wooden

On the evening of April 17, 1973, fourteen Dassault Falcon 20s owned by a little-known startup company took off from Memphis International Airport and successfully delivered 186 packages to twenty-five U.S. cities by the following morning.

An idea that had first taken root eight years earlier in a term paper by a Yale University student now had taken flight across the darkened American skies. Eventually it reshaped an industry and set the standard for one of the most important goals of every business in the world—reliability.

Federal Express, the brainchild of Fred Smith, grew into a billion-dollar freight shipping business by making and keeping its promise to deliver each package "when it absolutely, positively has to be there overnight." Smith launched the overnight package industry on a single (and simple) promise that came to permeate the industry— unconditional reliability—and business leaders, understanding the importance of reliability, loved it.

Indeed, nothing is more basic, more foundational to business, than reliability. And nothing is more basic or more foundational to work ethic.

Brands rise and fall on reliability. We want the Chick-fil-A sandwich we buy in Birmingham to taste like the one we had in Boise. We want the watch we wear to tell us it's 5:19 p.m. when it is in fact 5:19 p.m. We want the e-mail we send to show up within seconds in the recipient's inbox. We want our car to start when we turn (or push) the ignition—not every fourth time, but every single time. And if these things don't deliver on their promise, then we deem them unreliable and look for something we can rely on to replace them.

That's why brands spend so much time, effort, and money trying to convince us that we can always count on them. Indeed, reliability is central to just about every advertising message you've ever heard. Look at the promises of reliability in renowned advertising slogans like "It Takes a Licking and Keeps on Ticking" (Timex), "It Keeps Going and Going and Going . . ." (Energizer), "It's Everywhere You Want to Be" (Visa), and "A Diamond Is Forever" (De Beers).

Whether overtly or subtly, all brands make a promise: you can count on me to snap, crackle, and pop; to provide relief from indigestion; to taste good; to earn you money on your investments; to provide high performance; to deliver your package overnight.

If the brand delivers on the promise, it grows and thrives in the marketplace. If it fails, it suffers. And if it fails consistently, it dies.

Toyota became the envy of the auto industry by producing vehicles that delivered reliability. At one point, the automaker used the slogan, "The best-built cars in the world." And it lived up to that promise by churning out reasonably priced, nice-looking cars that got good gas mileage and didn't cost much to maintain. Then, in 2009, reports surfaced that some Toyota models had problems with their brakes. Not only that, but the company appeared slow in addressing the problems. Toyota's reputation for reliability took a hit in the marketplace, and it had to regroup and begin reproving itself to the car-buying public.

Reliability and the Brand of Me

What holds true for automakers, investment counselors, restaurants, and overnight delivery services also holds true for people. Brands, products, services, and businesses aren't just the things we purchase or the companies from which we purchase them. They are the people behind the products and services; the people within the businesses; the people who make things and provide services. The flaw in any failed brand, product, service, or business, in fact, almost always points back to the people who developed, made, marketed, sold, or serviced it.

There is no business owner, leader, or manager in the world who wouldn't want his workers to consistently live up to the FedEx promise—that when it absolutely, positively has to get done, they will get it done. He wants them there and ready to work when they're schedule to be there.

We all understand that nobody is perfect, but instilling reliability into your young hires isn't about trying to make them perfect. It's about instilling within them the importance of consistently making every possible effort and going all out to deliver what is expected of them on schedule, every time.

Very few businesses—none that I can think of—can survive (much less thrive) with employees who consistently prove themselves unreliable. We want workers we can count on to show up on time and prepared to do their work, whether they will be supervised or not. Like a FedEx package, they arrive on time, but not just physically. They arrive mentally ready to do the job. They arrive with their heads in the game. If they are supposed to arrive with a brief or a completed project, they have it. And they deliver over and over and over throughout their shifts.

That's reliability, and if your people are deficient in this area, it doesn't much matter how great their workplace performance is; their value to you is greatly diminished.

The Struggle Against Developing Reliable Employees

Unfortunately, reliability has become a "yeah but" value among many Americans. It's one of those things we not only expect but demand from others while excusing ourselves from the pesky little responsibilities it might bring our way.

"You were five minutes late. Again."

"Yeah, but it was only five minutes. And I caught some bad traffic, you know? Besides, what's the big deal? You act like I'm the second gunman on the grassy knoll, for crying out loud. It's just five minutes, dude."

"You didn't complete the report."

"Yeah, but this is the first time in the last three weeks I didn't get it in on time. I've been way more consistent about getting mine in than Alex has. So before you get all up in my grill, go ask him if he's got his."

People who use this type of argument have likely been raised to believe that a good excuse can get them out of any situation, that authority figures rarely follow through on threats, and that citing examples of others who've also been irresponsible will make their actions less noticeable.

Many parents perpetuate the myth that individualism trumps responsibility, which is why employers hear a lot of the "I'm really a night person, so you shouldn't expect me to make it to work that early in the morning" and "I'm known for arriving fashionably late, and the party never starts without me" comments from young workers.

And for individuals whose primary lifeline is self-esteem, apologies become an appeasement rather than an expression of sorrow or regret. "I'm sorry you feel that way" and "I'm sorry you were disappointed" take the place of "I was wrong and I'll make sure it never happens again. Please forgive me."

There has also been a societal trend to water down standards for absenteeism. A Harris Interactive survey in 2010, for instance, found that 57 percent of salaried employees say they take sick days when they aren't really sick.[1] Calling in sick when you don't feel like going to work has become so commonplace that no one gives it much thought anymore: "Yeah, the fish looked like they were biting, so I took a sick day." There's a word for taking a sick day when you aren't really sick: *cheating*. But we've come to embrace any excuse as an acceptable one, and the more lenient and accepting we've become as a culture of excuses, the more young people have pushed the limits.

There is also a growing movement to let kids get up later, because this theoretically helps their bodies perform better. Some school districts, in fact, are setting back start times for middle school through high school.

"Teenagers are biologically programmed to prefer a later bedtime and a later wake-up time, so it is not surprising that they struggle with early school start times," Dr. Heidi V. Connolly, chief of the division of pediatric sleep medicine at the University of Rochester Medical Center in New York, said in a July 2010 article by *HealthDay*.[2]

There's been a lot of research on this and much debate. And even though some of the evidence is compelling, I remain unconvinced. I believe that many parents have grown weary of their teens whining about bedtimes and are looking for justification to throw up the white flag.

Have teens' bodies suddenly changed? Are farmers able to get the chickens, pigs, and cows to sleep in until

---

1 "Employees Take Vacation, Call in Sick to Escape 'Holiday Hiatus'," commissioned by The Workforce Institute at Kronos Inc., and conducted by Harris Interactive, March 2010.

2 "Later School Start Times May Foster Better Students," by Amanda Gardner, *HealthDay News*, July 5, 2010.

their kids are ready to feed them? Do you think students in India and China are watching Hulu until all hours of the night and sleeping the day away? Me neither. Old Ben Franklin wasn't blowing smoke when he penned that "early to bed, early to rise" rap. And I bet he didn't write it at 2:00 a.m.

Creating the Foundation

So if businesses depend on reliability, and reliability originates with employees, then business leaders need to infuse reliability into their company cultures. The best place to start is by focusing on the significance of being reliable and taking great strides to make certain all of your people understand how important reliability is to you, how it embodies the values of the organization, and how it affects their future within the organization.

Reliability begins with showing up—being where you are supposed to be when you are supposed to be there. That's a foundational expectation that your customers have of you and that you have of your team members.

Developing reliable employees requires helping them see through the myths of popular culture. To borrow the phrasing from the beginning of the old show *ABC's Wide World of Sports*, you need to figure out how to make them experience the thrill of victory (being able to rely on someone to come through) as well as the agony of defeat (when someone they rely on lets them down). Through role-playing, discussion, or actual events that they experience while on the job, helping them see how reliability makes or breaks a business—and a career—is absolutely crucial.

Obviously, this starts with setting clear expectations

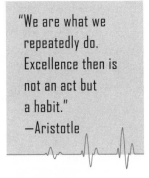

"We are what we repeatedly do. Excellence then is not an act but a habit."
—Aristotle

for each worker and then holding tight to those standards. There always come times when good managers make exceptions to the rules, but boundaries are worthless if they aren't consistently enforced. That means you need to think through your expectations for reliability, including the consequences when people are unreliable and the rewards for those who prove their dependability.

Instilling Reliability

Before you can instill any degree of reliability, you'll probably have to invest some time deprogramming the "yeah but" thinking. "Yeah but" may have gotten them through high school, worked on the coach to get them out of soccer practice, and even helped them navigate their dating life, but they need to learn that it doesn't fly in the workplace. They may not understand why they can't take Thursdays off, call in sick when they don't feel like working, or leave a little early when they've got a hot date. You've got to wake them up to realities of reliability in business, and do it in a way that they'll internalize for the long haul.

The best way to get them to relate the importance of being dependable and accountable is to use an analogy with which they can identify. For starters, ask them how frustrated they get when a cell phone call drops or when their Internet connection drags. Ask them why they choose one online source over another, and whether price is the only criteria. Do they care if their connection drops out every ten minutes? Ask them what happens when they make a reservation and the restaurant doesn't take it down or loses it. Let them feel the weight of unreliability, and intentionally build a gripe session around it so they feel free to vent about other people and other brands that have let them down. Resist the temptation to jump in, and conclude with a lesson.

Rather than waiting until they disappoint you to scold them, pick a time when there hasn't been an infraction to start a conversation that concludes with an agreement on the value you *both* place on reliability.

Be careful to use only one or two leading questions. You don't want to telegraph where you're taking the conversation, because they might quickly put up some defenses. But once you both agree how frustrating it can be to depend on someone only to be completely let down because he "spaced out" or couldn't get his car started, you'll find an easy transition in getting them to take an objective look at reliability as it applies to their personal brands.

Leveraging the Flipside

A totally different way to engage them in this conversation is to cite examples of extreme reliability. For instance, every sports fan in the world knows Cal Ripken, Jr.'s reputation for reliability. He was branded the "Iron Man" because he never missed a single start in a seventeen-year span. That's 2,632 consecutive games without taking a night off—a record baseball experts predict will never be broken! And Ripken wasn't only reliable to baseball; he was reliable to his team, the Baltimore Orioles. He played his entire twenty-one-year career for the O's, making the All-Star team nineteen times. Dependability, resilience, reliability, and loyalty all rolled up into one incredible athlete.

Or consider Brett Favre, who started his first game as a professional on September 27, 1992, with the Green Bay Packers and didn't miss a start until a separated shoulder kept him on the sidelines on December 12, 2010. That's an NFL record of 297 consecutive starts, not counting twenty-four playoff starts.

You think Brett Favre never felt like calling in sick? He even had a doctor's note on several occasions. In 2000, he started (and won) with a sprained left foot. In 2002, he started (and won) with a sprained lateral collateral ligament in his left knee. In 2003, he started (and won) with a broken thumb on his throwing hand. And in 2010, by this time age forty-one and playing for the Minnesota Vikings, he started with a broken bone in his foot. The Vikings lost that game to the New England Patriots, but only after Favre was knocked out of the game with a gash in his chin that required eight stitches. The next week he started and threw for a career-high 466 yards in a win over Arizona.

But if you want to bring it home and move on from celebrity athletes, tell your young people about Bob Knops, who worked at Twin City Wire in Eagan, Minnesota, until he retired at the age of eighty. Knops took two ten-minute breaks each day, plus thirty minutes for lunch, but otherwise he weaved wire for nine hours a day, five days a week. He never showed up late for work, and he never missed a day of work. Not once—in fifty-nine years!

His manager estimated that Bob weaved twenty-two million pounds of wire during his career, which is enough to stretch 25,000 miles.[3] Once you've told them about Bob, say, "You may not ever want to weave a single inch of wire, but can you imagine how Bob Knops's managers and coworkers felt about him? Talk about a guy you could depend on to have your back!"

Conversations centering around the incredible value most people place on reliability and the effect it has on an individual's personal brand can penetrate the conscious and subconscious minds of teens and young adults. Further, this technique opens the door for you to clarify your expectations when it comes to their reliability and assess what value they place on it.

Build Reliability in Their Schedule, from Back to Front

It's hard to argue with demographers when they say that your new labor force is a part of the most overscheduled generation in history. Wanting to account for their whereabouts every minute of every day, their parents have rushed them from one activity to another, making sure they got their homework done, made it to band practice, and led the food drive on the weekend.

While being active is admirable, a problem presents itself when employers discover their new employees are inept at managing their own schedules and are frequently late because they didn't plan for the unexpected.

---

3 "After putting in 59 years on the job, he's still a live wire," by Gail Rosenblum, startribune.com, April 28, 2009.

Smart employers don't further delay their maturity by planning for them; they tutor them in the art of managing workflow and being punctual. By assisting them in the creation of a reliability plan, you can wire them to look at their schedules in a linear fashion, starting in reverse with the deadline and then building in ample time for preparation, commuting, and unforeseen occurrences. This will help them avoid the last-minute syndrome and give them the confidence that they can—and will—be on time, every time.

Reliability in Your World

Okay, so you probably don't have a Cal Ripken, Jr. or a Brett Favre on your payroll, and you don't have a Bob Knops either. Those accomplishments are noteworthy precisely because they are unusual. But they do provide some inspiration for those days when we simply don't feel like getting out of bed because we stayed up late the night before to watch the last game of the World Series. I mean, if Favre can play professional football with a broken bone in his foot, surely you and I (and our workers) can get to work when we've got a headache, right?

I'm not suggesting that employees should work if they're sick or injured, but we all have times when we need to suck it up and go to work when we don't really feel like it. We need to do our best, even when we don't feel our best. Often, the biggest battle is defeating the "yeah but" excuse battle that is being fought in our own heads.

There are benefits to timeliness and being punctual

and dependable, and not just the benefit of staying on pace with a to-do list. The bigger benefit, and one that young workers can surely appreciate, is that it builds their reputations—their personal brands. Individualism often attacks work ethic, but it becomes an advocate when it comes to promoting a personal brand.

Members of the emerging workforce know the importance of their own brands. They know that their reputation matters and that they will have to promote themselves to clients, potential employers, customers, and investors to succeed. Teach them that if they have a proven track record for reliability, they will find the path much smoother. Help them connect the dots between their current reliability and their success in the future.

For instance, most young workers know they won't be a Bob Knops, sticking with one job and one company for nearly sixty years. In fact, on average, they'll change jobs seven times in their twenties.[4] And just about every time they change jobs, the potential new employer will call the current or previous employer. And the potential new employer will ask a series of questions that's almost sure to include this one: was this person reliable? You might be surprised to

> "Talent is cheaper than table salt. What separates the talented individual from the successful one is a lot of hard work."
> —Stephen King

---

4 "What Is It About 20-Somethings?" by Robin Marantz Henig, *New York Times*, August 22, 2010.

learn that most young people on your payroll aren't aware that this takes place, and they don't see how working a part-time or entry-level job is going to factor into their long-term career plans. At the right time and in the right way, you'll need to enlighten them.

Reliability isn't a value that only benefits the employer. It's a value that makes for a valued worker—one who will stay in high demand because she always delivers on her brand promise. Absolutely. Positively.

ADDITIONAL CONVERSATION STARTERS AND TIPS FOR INSTILLING RELIABILITY

During his championship years, Michael Jordan was the most widely recognized sports figure on the planet, and my son was a huge fan. From the time he was in third grade to right before his freshman year in high school, Zac (now twenty-seven) wanted nothing more than to talk about MJ every waking moment.

Zac wore black and red—the colors of the Chicago Bulls—almost every day, and nearly everything he owned had a 23 on it. He collected Michael Jordan books, Michael Jordan videos, and dozens of Michael Jordan hats. Once a year when the Bulls came to Denver, I'd pull out all stops to get us tickets so he could watch his hero dribble, pass, shoot, steal, and dunk his way to a victory over the hometown Nuggets.

So, during these years when Zac came to me with an excuse for why he couldn't cut the grass or why he couldn't complete his homework assignment, I'd occasionally play the Michael Jordan card.

"Really?" I'd say. "You can't get it done? What if you'd get to shoot hoops with Air Jordan himself, but he'd only play with you after you completed this task to perfection?" Then I throw in "and by the way, Jordan's leaving town first thing tomorrow morning! How fast could you get it done, then, little buddy?"

Most things aren't impossible if we have enough incentive, so most of us simply need to see reliability as something we can master through our own initiative. The Jordan conversation worked with my preteen son, but it's not going to get you much mileage with a fourteen- to seventeen-year-old who's not demonstrating reliability. Try this one on, instead:

"Let's say _____ (use the name of their favorite recording artist) is coming to town for a concert. And let's say a colleague of mine at work has connections and promises me that she can get free passes for you and a friend to go. But these aren't just regular passes. In fact, she can hook you up with two front-row seats with back-stage passes so you can meet and hang out with the band. And it comes with a limo to the concert, to the after-party with the band, and back to your house when the evening is finished.

"Sounds good, right? Here's the catch. To get these tickets, you and your friend both have to show up at the parking lot of the convenience store three blocks from your house at 1:52 a.m., and you both must be wearing fuzzy, pink slippers and bathrobes. That's it. That's all you have to do to go spend an incredible evening with _____.

"So what are the chances you'll show up at 1:53 or later? Zero, right?

"But guess what: your friend fell asleep while playing a video game and got there at 1:55 a.m.—three minutes late. And because of that, neither of you get the tickets."

Then shut up. Let it sink in. Better yet, let them respond in a snarky way and see how quickly they back themselves into a hole. You see, it's important to get your kid, your student, or your young worker to think about the implications of reliability, and there's no better way than to put them into a scenario where they have to bear the consequences of someone else's irresponsible actions.

Here are a few additional conversational questions you might use, or build on, to get a dialogue started with a teen or a young adult:

- Name the three most dependable people in your life. What makes you certain you can count on them? How would you feel about them if they let you down?

- What hurdles must you overcome in order to show up for work on time?

- If you added up the time it takes for every task you must do to get ready and get to work on time, what time would you have to begin the process?

- How much time do you build in to your schedule when coming to work to account for those crazy things that always seem to pop up at the worst possible moment—traffic jams, not being able to find your keys, or spilling mustard on your shirt?

- Describe a time when you felt your reliability made a positive difference for a friend, a boss, or a coworker. What was the end result?

- Think of an advertising slogan that describes your personal brand. If your current or former teachers, coaches, managers, and friends heard this slogan and were asked to think of a person they knew who fit that description, would your name be the first to pop into their head? If not, what can you do to make certain that you develop your brand so that everyone who meets you from this moment forward thinks of you that way?

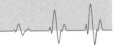

Universal Sandbox Values	Employers Want	Work Ethic Markers
Play nice, smile, and be polite	Positive, enthusiastic people	Positive Attitude
Be prompt	who show up on time	Reliability
Look your best	**dressed and prepared properly**	**Professionalism**
Do your best	go out of their way to add value/do more than required	Initiative
Obey the rules	play by the rules	Respect
Tell the truth	are honest	Integrity
Say *please* and *thank you*	give cheerful, friendly service	Gratitude

CHAPTER 7

PROFESSIONALISM

"You moon the wrong person at an office party and suddenly you're not 'professional' anymore."
—Jeff Foxworthy

Lynda did a double take when she noticed a young administrative assistant returning to her cubicle from the company break room.

As a senior executive in the human resources department of a large corporation, Lynda was no stranger to dealing with challenging employees. Her experiences told her she was about to take a stroll down Exasperation Lane, so she sighed inwardly as she walked toward the admin's desk.

Cami, the twenty-six-year-old payroll assistant, was wearing a low-cut blouse that exposed a sizable portion of her midriff. "It looked like the top half of a bikini from a *Girls Gone Wild* video," Lynda later told me.

It was a "casual Friday," so the rules were slightly

relaxed. Rather than business or business casual, employees in the corporate office were permitted to wear "appropriate" denim jeans and complementary logoed shirts or blouses from the official company catalogue of merchandise.

Lynda, like most experienced HR professionals, knows that when you relax company standards and allow for personal interpretations and various degrees of modifications and exceptions, you're opening the door to an avalanche of problems. Clearly, Cami had pushed the boundaries too far, and Lynda wasn't about to turn a blind eye to such a blatant infraction of the company's dress policy.

"I told her she wasn't dressed to code," Lynda told me. "Then I told her I would not send her home this time, but that she needed to put on a jacket to cover up her blouse."

The conversation didn't end there, however.

"Instead of apologizing and following my directive," Lynda said, "she started arguing with me."

"There's nothing wrong with what I have on," Cami said. "It's an expensive blouse, and I've gotten several compliments on it already."

"You need to be a professional," Lynda countered. "You're clearly out of code."

"That's ridiculous," Cami argued. "I work in a cubical. No one even sees me."

The argument escalated for several minutes until Lynda ran out of patience and sent Cami home for the afternoon without pay.

It's Not Personal—It's Business

Stories like Lynda's, unfortunately, are as common as

e-mail spam. Every company that employs teens and young adults wrestles with the boundaries of professionalism. How do you get the emerging workforce to set aside, if only temporarily, individual expression in favor of representing you and your organization without completely zapping them of their enthusiasm, creativity, and energy?

A professional, quite simply, is someone who understands and represents the organization's best interests, even when that means sacrificing personal preferences. Sometimes preferences line up squarely with the organization's needs, but often, especially for the emerging workforce, they don't. A professional puts the job ahead of personal desires. That means respecting her employer's culture, but it also means acting in the organization's best interests in ways that typically aren't covered by company policy.

Professionalism isn't just what a worker does, but how she goes about doing it. How she conducts and presents herself—the way she dresses, her body language, her tone of voice, the words she chooses, her hygiene—all define her persona and become a display of her professionalism, or lack thereof.

The biggest frustration many leaders experience with the emerging workforce comes from a seeming unwillingness to dress and act like professionals. I hear this from leaders and managers all the time, and it doesn't matter whether they're talking about blue-collar or white-collar workers. I hear it from people in the service industry, the medical industry, the financial services industry—every industry that counts on the emerging workforce can relate to this frustration.

The examples of "unprofessionalism" I hear about

most often—and I doubt any of these will shock you—generally fall into one of the following categories:

Appearance. The emerging workforce values fashion, which means you might have workers in baggy pants or jeans so tight you can read the dates on the change in their pockets. Either way, if it's not within the organization's dress code, it's not professional. Then there are the issues of tattoos and body piercings, hygiene, hairstyles, and the use of makeup. And don't think this is just a problem for those who employ low-wage, frontline workers. In 2010, a Citibank worker filed a lawsuit claiming she was fired because she dressed too sexy. Later that same year, Swiss banking giant UBS gave employees at five of its offices a forty-three-page dress code that detailed what its staff could and couldn't wear.

Language. Profanity, vulgarity, and obscenity are commonplace in the vocabulary of many members of the emerging workforce, and all too often they don't turn it off or even dial it down when they get to work. Many of them also seem to lack volume control, and some talk at hyperspeed. The result: You can't help but hear something that isn't meant for your ears. Finally, too many workers put too little effort into written communication. Out of sloppiness or ignorance, they use poor grammar and misspell words, and it reflects poorly on them and their employers.

Manners. This big umbrella covers common courtesies. Are your workers opening doors for others? Allowing others to speak without interruption? Calling their supervisors "Mr." or "Ms." until given permission to go with a first name? Do they go to business lunches and talk with their mouths full of food? Do they take a call or respond to a text when they're in the middle of a conversation with a coworker or customer? Do you sometimes wonder if they were raised in a barn?

Overtness. This shows up in a variety of forms. Anyone that has an opinion now has a platform to share it, thanks to the advent of social media. They've been raised to believe that if they have something to say or an interesting take on a subject or popular topic, they'd be depriving the world if they didn't "put it out there." This mentality compels many young people to post tasteless, thoughtless, and inappropriate comments and photos to sites like Facebook and Twitter. And if the posts happen to slam their boss or their employer, many young people just say, "Oh well." We need to respect the insights and opinions of our emerging workforce, but requiring public schools to bring back courses on etiquette, critical thinking, and self-control is not a terrible idea.

> "Treat people as if they were what they ought to be and you will help them become what they are capable of becoming."
> —Johann Wolfgang Von Goethe

Ultimately, these examples—and I suspect you have many others of your own—are all about workers who aren't separating personal attitudes and behaviors from their professional lives. When they cross the line into actions that affect your workplace and your company's image, you've got to be prepared to redraw that line in indelible ink.

The Fight Against Professionalism

There's been a movement over the past twenty or thirty years toward the "decompartmentalization" of life. The idea behind decompartmentalization is that the positive values and character you see in me in a professional setting should be the same ones I display at my church, in my home, or with my friends. In other words, I should be honest, caring, and helpful, regardless of the setting. I shouldn't "love my neighbor" on Sunday and scam her out of her life's savings on Wednesday.

This works great in matters of integrity, but it becomes problematic when it's taken out of context. And nowhere is decompartmentalization more unwelcome than in the workplace. You *want* people to compartmentalize their personal life and leave that compartment at home.

I believe it's important to be authentic and remain true to one's self, but that doesn't mean we're all supposed to let our hair down and be causal whenever the mood strikes. As stated in Ecclesiastes, there's a time to wear dress slacks and a sport coat and a time to wear Spandex biking shorts and a dew rag. (Okay, I was paraphrasing.) What I really want to wear in either situation is not the first consideration.

So why do so many workers fail to understand what seems like such an obvious distinction?

The heart of the issue is that younger workers often see professionalism—the kind most businesses seek—as an affront to their personal identities. *I can't do that and stay true to myself,* they think. The way they dress, speak, and act defines them, and they resent and rebel against anything or anyone that suggests they change who they are, even momentarily.

To understand this and better deal with it, we first must understand that the emerging workforce has been raised in a culture that sends conflicting messages about their appearances.

They are told, for instance, that they should feel comfortable discovering and living out their unique expression of self and that the rest of society shouldn't judge them based on their outward appearance. The obnoxious characters often become the heroes, and in some television shows and movies, like *Ugly Betty*, *Jersey Shore*, and *Glee*, the biggest stars are typically the loudest, lewdest, and most scantily clad.

The world of pop culture celebrates uniqueness, and defying conventionality is the quickest way to get noticed. Standing far apart from the crowd, however you choose to do it, gives you a competitive edge.

Nonconformity is the new normal. If each worker is his own brand, he must be unique. He can't dress just like anyone else. He can't even have a name like anyone else. If his parents didn't take care of that by giving him a name that looks like it came from an ophthalmologist's eye chart, then he's obligated to give it a twist. Samuel becomes S-cat or Slam-u-L. A friend of mine was at a charity event and asked a child his name. Without pause, the child, no more than seven-years-old, responded, "D-Money."

Rappers, led by Ice-T, Snoop Dog, and Eminem, have paved the way for anyone to make up words. There are even websites that translate "gangsta" language into regular English. *Fo shizzle*, folks. Then there's texting lingo, u no? Fashion trends still follow celebrities, but now anyone and everyone is a celebrity, and much of their fashion comes straight from prisons (baggy pants, for instance) and urban gang cultures. And then there are the body piercings, tattoos, and spiked-hair, colored-hair, and no-hair looks.

INK AND HOLES

- 38 percent of Millennials (ages eighteen to twenty-nine) have at least one tattoo.

- Of those who have at least one, 50 percent have between two and five tattoos. And 18 percent have six or more.

- 32 percent of Gen-Xers (ages thirty to forty-five), 15 percent of Boomers (ages forty-six to sixty-four), and 6 percent of Silents (ages sixty-five and older) have at least one tattoo.

- Of those older than thirty who have at least one tattoo, 47 percent have just one and only 9 percent have six or more.

- Nearly one-fourth (23 percent) of Millennials say they have at least one piercing somewhere other than an ear lobe. Only 9 percent of Gen-Xers and 1 percent of Baby Boomers have one.

Source: "Millennials: A Portrait of Generation Next" by the Pew Research Center, 2010

Advertising and marketing—which have grown significantly with the advent of the Internet, smartphones, and the corporate branding of everything from sport stadiums to water bottles—combine with Hollywood's long-standing drive to shape new trends. So messages about individuality hit us nonstop from all directions. No wonder young workers arrive in the workplace saying, "My identity is wrapped up in how I look and the way I talk, and I don't think I should have to change my outward appearance for the sake of a job. You should accept me for who and what I am."

And what if they go along with the manager's silly rules for, say, wearing a uniform, complete with a company hat? Chances are, they will twist the hat or turn it backward, sag the pants, and untuck the shirt (which is either two sizes too small or two sizes too large). Anything to make them appear as if they're leading your company's stealth image revolt.

Their message: *I have to make this uniquely mine or I'll lose me and become you.*

As millions of young Americans seek ways to prove their uniqueness, they expect the world around them to look on with a neutral or approving eye. *Don't judge me*, they'll say. Except that that's exactly what they want, if not from their manager at work, then from their peers. *Judge me to be cool*, is what they really want. *Otherwise, don't judge me.*

So while they are busy shaping their outer selves and watching television shows about plastic surgery or tattoo shops so they can avoid conforming to the latest trends, they're also digesting—and promoting—the ideal that *what really matters* is what's on the inside.

The inevitable train wreck occurs when these workers, shaped by all these mixed messages, show up in all their nonconformity for a job in which the manager asks them to dress a certain way, speak a certain way, and act a certain way.

Getting the emerging workforce to dress and act professionally is far easier, of course, when you hire professionals from the get-go. But as we've already established, the labor pool isn't exactly chock-full of young people who fit that job description; in fact, the pool may seem more like a swamp overrun with radicals determined to call the shots themselves.

Your discontent with the lack of professionalism among young workers may have you hiring more and more based on *potential*. You may have to rely on an online personality assessment to tell you when you've found someone who is moldable. You may feel that if you get a good raw prospect who comes from a good home, you can teach him the skills needed for the job and can more easily convince him to stop texting when he's talking to a customer. However you see it, this issue demands your attention. You can't leave something as important as professionalism out of your hiring considerations, and you certainly can't omit it from your training programs.

Clarity Is Crucial

With young employees, it's vitally important to clarify your expectations for professionalism on the front end, even before hiring them. Don't hand them a book of rules; instead, have a conversation that gives you an opportunity to explain what it takes to succeed in your organization, and allows them the freedom to respond to make sure they are on the same page.

Say things like "We never chew gum when we're working on the sales floor." "We don't use curse words when we're on the clock, even when we're just among coworkers." "We always end a transaction with a personalized expression of your gratitude that the customer chose to do business with us."

Whenever possible, include the context and reasoning for your expectations:

"It's not that I am down on gum. I enjoy it myself. But there's nothing more distracting to a customer than trying to concentrate on what you're telling him when all he sees and hears is a lot of chewing. That dings your image and makes us all look a little less classy."

"You know, when I'm out with the guys at a cage match, I get carried away and my language can get awfully colorful. But we're trying hard to distance ourselves from that kind of mob scene and maintain a respectful, professional environment around here. So we are death on the use of any words that you wouldn't use at your grandmother's Thanksgiving table. No exceptions, okay?"

When addressing something as important—and as controversial—as a dress code, don't simply describe it verbally or expect them to read it in the company handbook. Instead, show photographs of employees wearing both appropriate and inappropriate attire. This is inexpensive and very easy to do. Again, leave nothing to chance and don't surprise them with the specifics of your dress code after they've been hired and are making their way through your orientation.

Clarity during the hiring and on-boarding processes becomes the ounce of prevention that is worth the pound of cure. Unfortunately, many members of the emerging workforce arrive already in need of a cure. When it comes to professionalism, you see, the biggest problem comes when workers put themselves in the Cheating Quadrant. They know what's expected and choose not to do it— sometimes even if their manager is watching. What you and I see as insubordination, they might see as testing the limits or simply expressing themselves.

So while increasing their cognizance remains a high priority when it comes to professionalism, the bigger issue is usually motivation. How can you motivate compliance to standards that push employees to temporarily abandon their individuality?

For starters, make your rules relevant to them. It would be impossible to overemphasize this point: they will not consistently adhere to the "what" without first understanding the "why" behind it. For example, as you show photos of employees in proper and improper dress, tell them how your dress code came to be, how often it's reviewed, and the process for amending any part of it. That may seem like overkill to you, but it will speak volumes to your employees and let them know that you take appearance very seriously. It also prevents them from playing the "Oops, I didn't know" card in the future.

Teens and twentysomethings know that if they sign up for a part in a play, they are expected to dress and act the part. They wouldn't perform Othello in sunglasses, a

T-shirt, and cargo pants. And when they sign up for a job, they must dress and act the part of the employee and wear the "costume" the way it appears in the script.

This is where you can drive home the point I made a little earlier: there is a time to wear a coat and tie and a time to wear biking shorts. To them, this should mean that there might be a time to dress like a gangsta, talk like a Valley girl, or act like they have nothing in the world to do other than text their friends, but that time isn't when they're at work.

Steve, a VP of operations for a national drug store chain, shared a story he used during his management days when his young frontline employees would push the envelope on his very strict dress code. When called out because of their appearance, they'd pull out the "What I wear doesn't affect who I am or what I can do" argument. So Steve concocted an anecdote that helped him expose the faulty logic of that argument in a way that was very real to his young employees. He'd get them to close their eyes and take a deep, relaxing breath. Then, while their eyes were closed, he'd say to them,

> Imagine you're in the hospital and about to go into the operating room for a rather delicate surgery. It's a life-or-death type of surgery; so even though the doctors have assured you that your prospects are good, you still had to sign a bunch of waivers regarding the possible bad outcomes.
>
> You're trying to keep a positive attitude as the nurses take you into the operating room. And you're trying to relax when you're told the anesthesiologist has entered the room. "He'll stand behind

you and monitor your vitals and your medications," you are told. "He'll make sure you have just the right levels of anesthesia to keep you under, but not to cause you harm. It's his responsibility to keep your heart beating throughout this procedure."

"Yo, yo, wat up, dawg?" You hear his voice behind you, and you look up to see . . . an unshaved guy with numerous nose and lip piercings and the words "Life is Overrated" tattooed on his forehead. He smiles a somewhat twisted smile, and you feel and smell his warm, stale breath as he begins putting a mask over your face. "Let's get this party started!" he snarls.

So, what are you doing about now?

Anyone in their right mind would tell you they're yanking out their IV and sprinting toward the hospital exit. That's when Steve would casually insert,

"So, you're telling me that you do make judgments about others based upon their appearance, correct?"

"Usually, the discussion would end about there," Steve said.

Rockin' Professionalism

A pop-culture clothing shop in the mall will have a very different dress code than a high-end jewelry store, not because the owners are casting judgments about personal style, but because certain styles work better for selling $10,000 bracelets than for selling $30 gothic-style

T-shirts. And while you might want your workers wearing a $5,000 Armani suit if you run a brokerage firm on Wall Street, that attire wouldn't be appropriate for a waiter at a Hard Rock Café.

In fact, Hard Rock International, the international conglomerate that now includes hotels, retail stores, and casinos, as well as its original rock 'n' roll–themed cafes, provides an interesting case study of how professionalism can play out among the emerging workforce.

Jim Knight, senior director of training and development for the company's corporate university, the School of Hard Rocks, lovingly describes the company as "an Island of Misfit Toys." It's where people who often don't fit anywhere else find comfortable, long-term employment that brings out the best in them. But that doesn't mean they can check their professionalism at the door. Hard Rock's employees are allowed to express their individuality, but they must do so within the context of professionalism.

Employees at Hard Rock, for instance, may be able to grow a beard or sport a purple mohawk, but they are required to go about it a certain way. They need to have a plan for their "look" that meets Hard Rock's hygiene and appearance standards. They can't look as if they simply rolled out of bed and forgot to shave or comb their hair that day. And while managers may not take issue with a waiter who resembles Ozzy Osbourne, they won't tolerate any server who mumbles incoherently like Ozzy when taking a customer's order.

All Hard Rock's managers have expectations about hygiene, appearance, quality of service, manners, and reliability—all the things that make up work ethic. So even though Hard Rock looks, feels, and is culturally cool, it can't turn its young employees loose to dress, talk, or act any way they choose.

If you're dismissing this example by thinking that you can't allow your employees to dress in rock attire or relax your standards to meet the demands of your young workers, you're missing the point. Hard Rock's managers enforce rules, standards, and policies that may even be stricter than yours. But they know who they are, and they are experts in finding people who are going to live out their values.

There are no surprises for their new hires. They aren't ambiguous about what they demand. And by living out the underlying value of respecting individuals for who they are, the organization radiates a culture that celebrates individuals while still embracing professional standards. That's how they take thousands of workers with a bent toward nonconformity and get them to conform to and deliver the highest measures of professionalism.

"When you take mohawked, tattooed, and body-pierced Millennials and allow them to work in an industry that probably would not have given them a shot elsewhere because of the way they looked, acted, and thought, and then you treat them with respect, magic happens," Jim told me. "You get loyalty. Loyalty like you would never believe. It's why we are still fond of handing out Rolex watches at ten years to every employee who sticks around. It's an expensive reward, and we're proud to do it."

And Jim tells me that most of the accountability to maintain professional standards comes from the front-line employees, not the managers. The professionalism is ingrained in the culture and the workers self-police it to an extremely high degree—they understand that professionalism is important to the greater good of the organization. What the individual wants and feels are important, but not more important than the good of the whole.

That's what it means to *represent* an organization, and that's why it's critical to have an organization anyone would be proud to represent. The more you relax your standards, the more your employees will live down to them (or below them). If you cut corners, they will cut corners. But if you demand excellence at every turn, professionalism will become a huge part of your culture.

Whether you manage a Hard Rock Café, an Apple store, or a branch office of Wells Fargo, you want your frontline workers to *represent* you in a manner that keeps with the organization's high standards and the expectations of your customers or clients.

In the political world, governments assign ambassadors to represent the country's interests before foreign governments. These ambassadors have to dress, speak, and act in ways that present a positive image for their country. And they have to dress, speak, and act in ways that honor the foreign country. America wouldn't get far in its dealings with an Islamic country by sending a woman wearing shorts, tennis shoes, and a halter-top to speak about critical nuclear arms reductions.

When workers realize and embrace the idea that part of their job is to help promote the image of the organization rather than their personal image, they are more inclined to dress the part, speak the part, and act out the part that the job requires. That's professionalism in its truest sense.

ADDITIONAL CONVERSATION STARTERS
AND TIPS FOR INSTILLING PROFESSIONALISM

As we've discussed, the best time to address work ethic with an employee is before he becomes an employee, and you can dive particularly deep when it comes to professionalism. This provides a baseline for addressing problems as they arise.

When those problems arise, it's good to have a one-on-one conversation with the employee. And this often goes over better if the conversations aren't always a matter of discipline. Find time to sit with employees individually for brief periods when you have no agenda other than just asking how things are going and learning a little more about who they are as a person. This helps establish trust and respect, which becomes particularly key when addressing more sensitive issues.

When you have those one-on-one conversations, here are some sample questions that might help open doors or drive a discussion:

- Who is your favorite professional athlete? What makes him or her a professional as opposed to an amateur? In addition to natural skills or talents, what makes him or her "more professional" or a "better professional" than other athletes?

- Would you wear your work uniform (apron, name badge, hat, etc.) to a Lil Wayne or a 50 Cent show? Then why would you wear your rap concert apparel to work, or even remotely mix the two styles?

- What does the way you dress show your employer about what you think of your job?

- What part did professional standards—the way you dress, act, and speak—play in the types of companies you picked when looking for a job?

- Tell me what you think the corporate image is for each of these companies:
  - Ralph Lauren
  - MetLife
  - Chili's
  - Waste Management

- If you were writing a dress code for an entry-level sales position for each of those organizations, what would it look like?

- How important is it to your self-image for your peers to think you dress "cool"?

- How would you feel if one of your parents lost a job because they had poor hygiene?

- What are some reasonable nonnegotiables for professionalism in your current work (dress, speech, hygiene, etc.)?

Universal Sandbox Values	Employers Want	Work Ethic Markers
Play nice, smile, and be polite	Positive, enthusiastic people	Positive Attitude
Be prompt	who show up on time	Reliability
Look your best	dressed and prepared properly	Professionalism
Do your best	**go out of their way to add value/do more than required**	**Initiative**
Obey the rules	play by the rules	Respect
Tell the truth	are honest	Integrity
Say *please* and *thank you*	give cheerful, friendly service	Gratitude

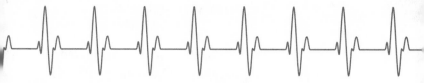

CHAPTER 8

INITIATIVE

"If a man is called a streetsweeper, he should sweep streets even as Michelangelo painted, or Beethoven composed music, or Shakespeare wrote poetry. He should sweep streets so well that all the hosts of heaven and Earth will pause to say, 'Here lived a great streetsweeper who did his job well.'"
—*Martin Luther King, Jr.*

Thunder Valley Motocross Park sits along the western edge of Denver in Lakewood, Colorado, an otherwise quiet suburban city nestled against the foothills of the Rocky Mountains.

When the snow melts each spring, hundreds of riders don multicolored protective gear and push the limits of gravity and sanity as they roar around the track at one of the nation's top motocross parks.

All spring, all summer, and late into the fall, they practice and race and practice and race, the young and the old, the amateurs and the pros, the boys, girls, men, and women. They spend thousands of dollars on equipment, not to mention travel expenses, and they lovingly care for their bikes before driving them hard as they fly up, over, and around the dirt track at the 1,300-acre park.

Some weekends, more than a thousand riders show up. They come for the challenge of driving a motorcycle so fast that it often soars to unimaginable heights. They come for the chance to push the envelope on the extreme. They come for the trophies that go to the victors. They come because they want to go all out.

Now, imagine the reaction you'd get if you looked any of these daredevils in the eyes and said, "Are you trying to avoid being the slowest rider out here today?" Of course they aren't. All of them arrive and race with the same objective—to become the best on the track and make a name for themselves.

Less than fifteen miles away from the motocross park, a different breed of adventurers pushes the limits. The Denver Skatepark is one of the largest of its kind, with a half-dozen bowls and a street terrain area that features banks, stairs, rails, planters, curbs, ledges, and a "snake run" to challenge the dozens of skaters who show up whenever the weather is good (or close enough to good).

The park isn't far from my office, so I'll sometimes fix a sandwich for lunch and spend an hour or so watching these fearless riders perform stunts on boards and skates that, to me, seem impossible. Each young skater seems hell-bent on defying the laws of physics to a degree that surpasses the person who went previously. And a painful fall never acts as a deterrent to that mission.

Like the motocross riders, the skateboarders remind me of the time when my son and a couple of his friends formed a band. They were in the eighth grade, and the trio—No Cash Value, as they were known—set out to win the school's battle of the bands. They poured themselves into it, practicing hour after hour with a determined focus of winning that competition. I'd never seen my son go "all in" on any endeavor or project, but with this he seemed possessed by a desire to be the best.

I think about the motocross fanatics, and the skateboard junkies, and the garage band maniacs, and I wonder: how many of those people would bring that same drive, sweat, passion, and creativity to a part-time job in the local mall, at the grocery store, or at the taco house in the strip mall? Then again, how many adults bring that same level of committed enthusiasm to their careers in sales, law, finance, education, construction, or medicine?

In the drive and passion of the three examples above, we see the essence of a critical component for being a superstar in the workplace—initiative. Pick any sport, hobby, or interest, and you can witness a tribe of enthusiasts pledging countless hours to improving their skills and making their mark. They push themselves above and beyond what's required—they show initiative because it's the first step toward victory or the rush of adventure.

The Fight Against Mediocrity at Work

Unfortunately, the prevailing mentality among many workers in America looks nothing like the sense of pride and passion you find at the motocross track, the skate park, or a middle school band competition.

Instead of working hard, taking calculated risks, and trying to get noticed for positive achievements, the workers I'm describing settle for the MDR (minimum daily requirements). They work just hard enough to avoid getting into trouble, trying to stay under the radar to avoid getting fired. They live to "thank God it's Friday." There isn't much evidence that they want to move up or be the best at their jobs.

When you see these types of uncommitted, sloppy young workers, it's tempting to write them off as incompetent, lazy, or uncaring—as if this is the best they have to offer and they aren't capable of better performances. But don't blame the new generation for a problem that's been growing for years. The emerging workforce takes careful note of role models who may put in long hours at work but who don't always bring much passion or enthusiasm to their work. Young people hear their parents and teachers frequently complaining about work and trying to find ways to avoid tasks so they, too, can reserve their best for hobbies and recreational pursuits.

I've delivered more than one hundred opening-day faculty and staff in-service programs for school districts throughout the United States and Canada, and the conversations in the lobbies prior to these presentations sound like carbon copies of each other. One educator walks up to another and says, "How was your summer?" And the other inevitably replies, "Too short." Translation? "I wish I didn't have to be back at work because I'd much rather still be working on my garden, reading fiction, or playing golf." How great is class going to be for students if their teacher doesn't really want to be there?

This "I'd rather be fishing" mentality does little to inspire initiative in the hearts and minds of the emerging workforce. And over time, many young people have adopted a "why bother" attitude when it comes to proactively making things better for themselves or the world around them.

Am I painting with too broad a brush here? Perhaps. But consider John Mayer's 2006 hit "Waiting on the World to Change,"a sort of theme song for Gen Y indifference. That song helped Mayer win a Grammy Award for Best Male Pop Vocal Performance, and the album it appeared on went platinum. The lyrics tell of young people who are "misunderstood" and who have no means to change the world around them. Their response? They "wait on the world to change."

You can look up the song's lyrics online if you like, but the title should give you an idea of the overall theme. The song is a "lovely and anger-free ode to a vaguely dissatisfied generation," according to *The New York Times*. And *Rolling Stone* called it a "moving apologia for Gen Y's seeming 'apathy.'"

I'm no music critic, but I believe Mayer's "lovely and anger-free ode" that supposedly offers hope and a "moving apologia" for a generation's "apathy" does nothing but reinforce the stereotype of post–generation Xers as indifferent, lethargic, and entitled.

I wonder if Herbert Hoover somehow had this song in mind decades earlier when he said, "Words without actions are the assassins of idealism."

Up and At 'Em!

If your sons, daughters, students, friends, or employees are sitting and waiting for the world to change, it likely will pass them by. It will change, because it always does. And the passive can watch as others change it and reap the benefits of their efforts—financial benefits in some cases, but also the benefits of knowing they made a difference and left a legacy.

Will the upcoming generations show any initiative in rising to leadership, or will they take over by default (by the force of their sheer numbers) until real leadership fills the vacuum? You can't wait until you reach a position of power or authority to begin showing initiative, and that's why it's so important that members of the emerging workforce develop this component as early as possible.

> "Without ambition one starts nothing. Without work one finishes nothing. The prize will not be sent to you. You have to win it. The man who knows how will always have a job. The man who also knows why will always be his boss."
> —Ralph Waldo Emerson

The person with initiative doesn't settle for the minimum standards, much less wait for the world to change. This person wants to be the best at her work, because that's how she creates value for her employer and that's how she becomes valued. Her value is tied to the things she knows and the things she does that go above and beyond the job description. If there's a promotion available, she'll get it. If times get tough, she'll be the last person her employer lets go. And even if the business closes, she won't be out of work for long because she'll have what every employer wants—value.

As a friend of mine told his son, "There might come a time when the manager needs to thin the herd. You need to give him every reason to make sure his cuts don't include you."

Clarifying the Initiative You Want to See

If the emerging workforce is going to stop waiting on the world to change and start changing the world, it must embrace initiative. At the same time, the leaders of this dynamic, energetic, passionate, creative, and thoughtful generation can't sit around waiting on them to change.

Leaders lead. Leaders accept responsibility. Leaders take initiative and show the way. If that's what members of the emerging workforce are waiting on, then they should wait no longer. You, as a leader, must make the first move and show them the way—with every single component of work ethic.

This begins, again, with clarity, so if you want people to exceed expectations, then they need to have a clear understanding of (a) what the expectations are and (b) what they can do to exceed them. Sounds simple, but it's often overlooked or taken for granted.

New employees—and, at times, more veteran employees—need to know the baseline for excellence and how they can get above it. Say, "Here's your job. Here are the basic requirements for this job. Now, here are some things you can do if you've completed those essential tasks. And, by the way, if you see something else that needs doing and there's no one else to do it—do it!"

It may start with the actual job titles you assign. A young person hired as a "cashier," for example, may think all he has been hired to do is to ring up sales. Why would he ever think about picking up the stack of boxes that fell off the shelves in the aisle between the break room and the employee bathroom? *That's clearly a job for a stock clerk, not a cashier*, he thinks. And if there is a customer who needs assistance with a merchandise-related question, he might think, *Isn't that a job for a salesperson?*

Leaders clarify the value of initiative by showing their employees that everyone has a responsibility for adding value to the organization in any way they can. This shared responsibility creates team play and says to the employee, "We're all in this together."

But it's also important to clarify the limits of initiative. Let's say you run an adventure company that takes people white-water rafting on the upper Arkansas River. You hire a college student to help load the boats, and one day a group shows up early and says its ready to go. The boat captain, however, won't be there for thirty minutes. Your eager employee might show some initiative and say, "No worries. I'll take you down the river. Grab a life vest, load up, and let's go!" But he's not trained to navigate a raft full of novices down a fast-flowing river, so his initiative will likely wash ashore somewhere downstream with the paddles and the people.

Keep Their Minds in Your Business

Zaxby's, a chain of restaurants that sells chicken meals to guests in more than five hundred stores across the Southeast, gives its employees a list of peak activities and non-peak activities so that they know what to do when dealing with customers and what do when there are no customers in the store. The leadership provides clarity in the form of an action plan for slow times. No employee can ever say, "I have nothing to do."

Pal's Sudden Service, a nearly sixty-year-old chain of burger restaurants in Tennessee and Virginia, requires employees to submit two ideas each month on ways the company can improve its quality of service. As a result, the employees make a habit of looking for quality service. They have a heightened sensitivity to it; after all, they have to know what it looks like if they're going to suggest ways to improve it. And when young employees submit ideas that are good enough to implement, they are praised and rewarded for it, which energizes other young employees to follow suit.

Here's what the other side of that coin looks like: you hire a receptionist for your law offices, and on the first day you train her to answer the phone, transfer calls to the appropriate places, and take messages. The next morning you walk by and notice her sitting at the front desk posting comments to her Facebook page.

"Why are you reading?" you ask.

"Phones are all quiet this morning," she says.

"Okay, well, if no one is calling, you could clean the coffee pot," you tell her.

So the next day you come in and she's at the desk reading a romance novel.

"No one is calling and I've already cleaned the coffee pot," she explains.

Seeing such low-level initiative is frustrating, but you can't assume she learned how to perform in her job at home or at school. You need to help her see what adding value to your organization looks like. You need to make the scope of her responsibility and authority clear, and you need to tell her what she should do during slow periods. You also need to show her that contributing value to the organization will help her rise through the ranks and develop her resume of skills for her next job. So, it's to her advantage, not just yours, if she looks for or asks for new assignments when things get slow or if she simply sees an opportunity to make things better.

This process includes a degree of assessment. You need to know what she's doing and what she's capable of doing. Can she learn a new software program, for instance, and do data entry during her spare time? If so, make that training part of her workweek. As she gets to know the organization, ask her where else she thinks she can add value to the team, and then help her put some of those skills to use.

When people have a clear understanding of what's expected of them and of the things they can do to exceed those expectations, they still might not do it. They might look it over and say, "Nah, I'd rather coast" or "All the extra work doesn't appear to have any payoff for me." So, while they might have a generous portion of cognizance, they're deciding to pass on the compliance. This is where relevance, rewards, and radiating the values of work ethic come back into play.

Initiative Compliance

Initiative is relevant to the company because it prepares the worker for additional assignments and makes him invaluable to his current employer. It's relevant to the employee because it gives life to his goals and ambitions, and is the component of work ethic that makes an employee feel the most proud. The employee with initiative can say, "I did that without being told, and I know it made a difference." Initiative will also put him in great demand by future employers.

Even though they might not come to you begging for more work, your employees want to know how they can contribute value to the company. When you let them know that you have a problem you'd like their input on, you'd be amazed at the initiative they'll take in trying to help you solve it. Whether or not they hit on the right solution, getting their minds working toward finding solutions to problems and inviting their contribution takes them out of the automaton state and moves them into an entirely different mindset: "This is my business, too, and when I have an idea for making something better, or if I see a problem that needs fixing, I can add value to the company—and also make myself more valuable in the process." That's right where you want them—fully engaged with head, heart, and hands!

When they demonstrate initiative, reward it. You can applaud it on the spot. You can honor it during team meetings. You can acknowledge it in front of employees, clients, and customers. You can promote it in the media—both social and traditional. And you can straight-out pay for it by providing a bonus or promotion that says to your entire staff, "We're always on the lookout for people who put their mind—and elbow grease—to work around here."

Owning Boredom

The coolest thing about initiative is that it is the cure for one of the most common complaints young people have about their jobs: "I'm bored." Most jobs simply don't change fast enough for young employees. They want to learn faster and be promoted faster than most companies can accommodate. When they find themselves doing repetitive tasks day in and day out, they get bored and start looking for the escape hatch.

Instilling initiative in your young staffers enables them to own their boredom. What you're saying is, "When you are the best, the very best, unbeatable by anyone else in our organization at your tasks and your job, *then* we'll move you on. In the meantime, you need to know every single aspect of your job. Study the manuals, practice your skills, do an assessment of how we can train new employees in this area. Make it uniquely yours."

This causes young people to take ownership and feel like they can put their stamp on a job. The intrinsic rewards that come with this often surpass any perk or benefit you can give them and spill over into future assignments.

Initiative, like most components of work ethic, is contagious. When people see it in their leaders and their peers—when they see the rewards—they tend to try it for themselves. And the more it works for them, the more they make it a part of who they are. And the more they make it part of who they are, the more it radiates throughout the culture.

Pass the Passion

I started this chapter talking about the passion you see in motocross riders, skateboarders, and garage bands. And you might still wonder how to infuse that type of passion into the workforce at your clothing store, restaurant, factory, church, law office, school, medical practice, bank, home, or . . . well, whatever and wherever.

There is an undeniably strong link between passion and initiative, but it might not be the link you think. Passion doesn't fuel initiative; initiative fuels passion.

Most people want to go about it backwards. They want to let their passions propel their initiative. They want an emotion-driven life, but our emotions don't always lead us where we need to go or keep us where we need to be.

You won't produce heat in your fireplace by saying, "Once there's a fire, I'll put in some logs." You put the logs in and build a fire, and then you'll see some heat. Likewise, the passion you have for a job is directly related to the initiative you put into it. Many highly successful people in all walks of life have discovered that because they put a great amount of effort into their job, their job eventually becomes their passion. They didn't set out to be the

> "Fires can't be made with dead embers, nor can enthusiasm be stirred by spiritless men. Enthusiasm in our daily work lightens effort and turns even labor into pleasant tasks."
> —James Baldwin, American author

world's greatest carpet installer, data entry clerk, or fry cook; they just set out to be the best they could be while in their jobs, and the next thing they knew they were *awesome* at it!

My friend Bill Cordes calls this YOGOWYPI (pronounced yoga-whippy). It's a simple acronym for You Only Get Out What You Put In, and it makes perfect sense, especially when it comes to initiative. If you don't put some initiative into what you do, you won't see any passion.

And far too many of us dismiss a job or a task before we even know if we have a passion for it. I don't have a passion for motocross because I've never tried it. If I tried it with enthusiasm and a positive attitude, I might discover a passion for it. But I'd have to take the initiative and try it in order to find out.

If a young worker says, "I don't have a passion for selling shoes," the first thing he needs to do is show some initiative by making selling shoes a short-term passion. If he throws himself into it, does all he can to learn the business and make himself the best, and he still doesn't develop a passion for the job, that's fine. He has still improved his reputation for adding value to a job, made himself more hirable, and developed his work ethic in the process. And then he can do his boss and himself a favor and quit. She'll likely give him a good reference or help him find another position within the organization.

As a leader, you can help members of the emerging workforce by encouraging them to discover their passions. That starts by helping them develop ambitions that go beyond "not getting fired," helping them set goals to achieve those ambitions, and then explaining the initiative required to make those ambitions a reality.

> "If you put out 150 percent, then you can always expect 100 percent back. That's what I was always told as a kid, and it's worked for me so far!"
> —Justin Timberlake

Or they can just take a seat and wait for the world to change around them.

ADDITIONAL CONVERSATION STARTERS AND TIPS FOR INSTILLING INITIATIVE

Coaches worldwide tell their players to "take it one game at a time," and the cliché continues to stand the test of time because of its intrinsic value. We all do well when we focus on the task at hand. But we can live in the moment and take life as it comes while still preparing for the future and working with the big picture in mind.

To do that, we need a healthy sense of ambition and a strong commitment to initiative. To share that message in a meaningful way with young employees, talk to them about their short- and long-term goals, their personal mission and vision for life, and the practical steps that will help them get there.

One healthy activity for anyone who needs direction in life—which is all of us—is to think about and then write out personal vision and mission statements. A vision statement will help them articulate what they want to accomplish with regard to the various aspects of their life—physical, mental, financial, spiritual, etc. A mission statement is a specific targeted goal they have for success in one specific area. Encourage your employees to dream big. Graduating from high school or college isn't a mission statement. Owning your own company, or starting a nonprofit that builds houses for the poor in South Africa, or becoming governor of your state—those are big dreams.

Mission and vision statements provide a compass for decision making, making it easier to focus on and achieve goals without losing sight of the big picture or getting too caught up in the next challenge.

To get an employee started, give her some examples. Share your personal mission and vision statements with her (you do have those, right?). Then ask her some of these questions:

- What are you most passionate about?
- What do you care most deeply about in life?
- What gets you excited in life? What feels like it is never work?
- What person or people would you most like to emulate? Why?
- What drives who you are as a person?

- Describe a time when you went into something thinking you wouldn't like it and ended up developing a real love for it? It could be a task, a type of food, or a band someone recommended.

- What beliefs do you cherish and will never compromise on?

- What value will you derive from having a vision and mission statement?

- How does your vision statement (once written) align with your perceived image of yourself?

It's also helpful to build some dialogue more directly tied to the importance of initiative and ambition. Here are some examples:

- What does "initiative" mean to you?

- How does initiative relate to ambition?

- What role does initiative play in creating passion?

- What does having ambition show your company?

- How can you get excited about something that, at first, seems dull and boring?

- What are the benefits of showing initiative and having ambition?

- What is the fastest way to advance in your job?

- If you had to work in this field for the rest of your life, what could you do to put your stamp on it and become the king of the industry?

- What keeps you from being ambitious?

Finally, help your employee count the costs that come from a lack of initiative. Give the employee an example of a young worker who got a credit card and bought some Christmas presents, clothes, and a few high-tech gadgets and toys. Before realizing it, he ran up $3,173 in debt (the average credit card debt for a college student in 2009, according to a survey by Sallie Mae). With an interest rate of 18 percent, the worker will need nineteen years to pay that off if he pays the $15 monthly minimum. And the $3,173 in stuff actually will cost him $7,358.28. That means the $50 video game (that he won't even have in nineteen years) really cost more than $100. Or he could make higher payments—$80.24 a month—and pay it off in about five years, saving nearly $2,500.

Initiative is all about the discipline of investing now—putting in the effort, sacrificing, *doing more than the minimum*—rather than waiting for the world to change. It's about bucking the "play now, pay later" trend to do just the opposite: put in an investment of initiative and reap the benefits later.

Or, as my dad would say, "Pay now, play later."

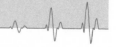

■■■

Universal Sandbox Values	Employers Want	Work Ethic Markers
Play nice, smile, and be polite	Positive, enthusiastic people	Positive Attitude
Be prompt	who show up on time	Reliability
Look your best	dressed and prepared properly	Professionalism
Do your best	go out of their way to add value/do more than required	Initiative
Obey the rules	**play by the rules**	**Respect**
Tell the truth	are honest	Integrity
Say *please* and *thank you*	give cheerful, friendly service	Gratitude

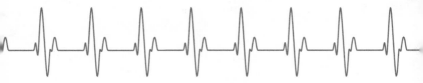

CHAPTER 9

RESPECT

"A culture of discipline is not a principle of business;
it is a principle of greatness."
—*Jim Collins*

The elation that came with landing my first "real" job faded pretty quickly when the walls of reality began closing in around me.

In the blink of an eye, I had traded in my adolescent freedom and autonomy for a Baskin-Robbins apron and cap. The carefree days of summer were replaced with schedules, dress codes, and evaluations—all things that demanded my attention and respect. At sixteen, I didn't want to answer to anyone other than me, myself, and I. Instead, I got a nagging boss who ordered me around like a drill sergeant at boot camp.

Rules. Regulations. Policies. Procedures. Standards. Requirements. Routines. Authority. Structure.

For what? A paycheck?

And to make matters worse, my parents insisted that 80 percent of each check go into my college fund: "You need an education if you are going to amount to anything, Eric" . . . "College isn't cheap, Eric" . . . "We aren't made of money, Eric." And as far as taking out a student loan, well, that wasn't even a remote consideration. "A Chester never goes into debt," my dad would say repeatedly. A job was simply something I *had* to have.

Actually, I was happy the folks let me pocket 20 percent, because that way I could save for a car. Now *that* represented freedom! My own set of wheels! With a car, why, I could . . . drive to work!

Don't get me wrong—I liked working at Baskin-Robbins. Cute girls frequented the place, and I got all the ice cream I could eat. But, man, I hated all the rules and regulations, and I couldn't stand my boss.

The thought of quitting entered my mind from time to time, usually arriving in a whisper or with a gentle nudge, but it never stayed around for long. My dad's voice countered with a high-volume shout that echoed through my head: "If you get fired, don't come home!" He wasn't trying to be a tough guy. It's just that his teenage years were spent trying to survive the Great Depression, and looking back, it now seems like his primary goal of father-hood was to make sure his only son knew how to find—and keep—a job. So even though I know he had my best interests at heart, he would have sided with my boss on any issue that ever arose.

I knew I had to suck it up and play by the company rules, and I had to put a smile on my face and accept the authority of the manager, even if I couldn't stand him.

The consequences for a lack of respect were too great—I wanted and needed the money, I didn't want to face my father's wrath, and I didn't want to look for another job in what at that time was a pretty tough job market.

Welcome to my world, circa 1973.

Even in a recessionary economy like we've recently experienced, most anyone in the emerging workforce who wants a job can find a job. The key word is *wants*. Many teens and young adults turn down or never even consider jobs they don't want, holding out for their version of the ideal. There's little or no pressure to learn the value of work or to save for the things they want to buy.

And if they take a job and don't like the rules or hate their boss, they face very few consequences for quitting or getting fired—except one they can't see until much later: that they missed a great opportunity to prepare themselves for life in the real world, a world where you don't always get things your way, and you don't always get to work for bosses you love.

In many states, employment law makes it difficult to fire an employee, even if he isn't complying with the basic rules that come with the job. And far too many parents, well intentioned though they might be, try to rescue their children from the learning experiences that come with challenging work and difficult-to-deal-with coworkers, employers, and customers.

After speaking at a recent annual convention for a large franchise of retail postal stores, one of the franchisees approached me to share that he had recently scolded a twenty-two-year-old employee who was caught napping on the job. "Her mother came about an hour later and really let me have it," he said. "She said her daughter had been up studying all night for a sociology exam and that I should be aware of these matters before saying anything to her that might leave an emotional scar."

Is it any wonder that so many young workers are not wired to respect rules or authority? Their helicopter parents have fueled their disregard for rules by jumping in at the first sign of trouble to defend them.

R-E-S-P-E-C-T, Find Out What It Means to Me

When I was researching this book and trying to define the labels for the tried-and-true ideals that mark work ethic, I recalled the many leaders and managers who had lamented their employee's disregard for authority. I felt strongly that this particular issue held great importance to helping young workers build lasting, valuable work ethic. Coming up with a one-word label for the value that would resolve the problem, however, wasn't easy.

I looked at words like *obedience*, *acceptance*, and *conformity* because they convey significant aspects of what I mean. Employers want their workers to conform to certain standards and expectations. They want their workers to accept and obey the rules, policies, and directives.

But none of those labels, I realized, fit perfectly, either because they held some negative connotation that might sidetrack my points or because they simply weren't a full expression of the ideal.

The more I thought about it, the more I felt that *respect* summed up this ideal. It has power. It's something we all want from others and something we all need to show.

The dictionary tells us that *respect* can be used as either a noun or a verb, and it literally means to "look back on" something or someone with an attitude of deference, admiration, or esteem. We all know people we respect because of who they are, how they live, and the accomplishments they've earned. Those people earned our respect. So it's natural to want to earn respect from others, and there's nothing wrong with that; we all should strive to earn the respect of the people around us.

In a work situation, however, respect can't begin or end there.

Every relationship at every job needs to start with the employee *giving* respect rather than setting out to earn it immediately. As employers and managers, we want our workers to show up with a basic respect for themselves, for the company's policies and standards, for the rules, for authority, for the goals and objectives of the company, and for their boss, coworkers, and customers.

It's not that your younger employees don't value respect. On the contrary, they know all too well what respect is, and, more important, the power it holds. They want respect; they never want to be "dissed"—not by their friends, not by their parents, not by their teachers, and certainly not by their employers. They live by the creed "He who has the respect has the power," and to them, respect is a prize that must be won. They crave it and will go to great lengths to get it, but when it comes to giving respect, they are stingy. They won't automatically respect a person simply because of her age, position, or title. They do not want to yield their power or put someone else in a position of control over them. In a strange reversal of the traditional dynamic between youth and age, they believe that they are owed respect automatically but that you have to prove yourself worthy of their consideration. In most situations, respect is bartered. "You respect me first," they seem to be saying, "and then maybe I'll respect you!"

Teaching them to internalize respect for others, for the task, and for the company—well, that's not easy, but accomplishing it brings tremendous value to employers and, in the long run, the teens and young people who are learning what it means to work.

You're Special—the Rules Don't Apply to You!

Because their interests and desires have been catered to by advertisers, media conglomerates, and even parents, teens and young adults are used to being sought after. Focus groups seek their opinions, marketers listen very, very carefully to what they think is cool and what they think is lame, and parents may spoil them rotten. And because their adulthood is being forced on them at younger and younger ages, in some cases they've needed more power to cope with an increasingly difficult world.

We promote things like independence, creative thinking, initiative, self-esteem, and "thinking outside the box" at the expense of equally—and sometimes more—important values such as respect.

Bestselling books with titles like *First, Break All the Rules* and advertising slogans like Outback Steakhouse's "No Rules, Just Right" perpetuate the notion that rules are a bad thing, and that you need to have the courage to stand up in the face of authority and be completely unconventional if you're going to succeed, have fun, and get ahead.

So music, movies, books, schools, friends, and even parents—all the major influencers of our lives—combine to hammer home messages that, when summed up, tell us that others must *earn our respect*, but that they should in turn *respect us* simply for who we are. Immediately, a double standard invades the way a culture and a generation views itself and its work.

To further complicate things, as mentioned previously, you are now employing people who were raised on an overdose of self-esteem. Remember, the heart of that message is to *esteem the self*, and that doesn't always result in healthy self-confidence or self-respect. When people feel they are above the law, or that a rule is made for someone who isn't as special as they are, compliance falls by the wayside.

Your ultimate aim, however, should not be to destroy or even minimize self-esteem, but rather to instill a sense of respect for others that supersedes self. This is not something that is done by imposing another rule; it's done through mentorship. It's important to bear in mind that while your parents had these conversations with you when your habits were being formed, this is probably new ground for the young people you're leading.

Up and Over Respect

As a leader, you have the ability to move people to the right, across the horizontal axis, by teaching them what respect is and why it is a nonnegotiable in your business.

And you move them up the vertical compliance axis when you show them why respect makes them stronger, not weaker, and why demonstrating respect will lead to more responsibility and a greater success for them.

Let's examine the three critical areas of respect you want to instill within your workers.

1. Workers must respect the work contract. Assume nothing. Clarity when it comes to their job-related obligations is not something you can take for granted. Your young workers need to know that they are entering an agreement to perform certain tasks for a certain amount of pay. If there are incentives, make them known. If there are standards, explain them. If there are rules, tell them what they are and why they exist. And, above all, if there are consequences for disrespecting the rules of the workplace, eliminate all ambiguity about them and make certain they are followed to the letter.

2. Workers must respect their managers and coworkers. When young, frontline staffers work with or for someone they don't like, they often must respect his position of authority and the role he plays within a team or an organization. They should know the procedure for resolving a workplace grievance, but also be made to understand that "tattling" on a supervisor or manager who they believe overstepped his authority is a practice that should only be used in rare and extreme circumstances. They must be taught how to separate personal feelings from workplace behavior, and be encouraged to think their way through tense situations with their bosses rather than spouting back each time they feel like they've been unfairly reprimanded or pouting when they feel they're due a pat on the back. These are not innate behaviors, and a little mentoring in these situations goes a long way.

3. Workers must respect the line between work and socializing. Your first bosses went out of their way to avoid hiring your friends because they wanted to keep you focused on work, not horsing around on the job. That's changed. Now employers know that to reduce turnover, it's important for young employees to work with people they like, so they try to hire a young employee's close friends. Working with friends makes work enjoyable, provides resources for support, and creates camaraderie and teamwork. But sometimes the nonwork dynamics of those relationships creep into work situations, and that can cause problems, or even chaos. To keep employees within the boundaries of acceptable workplace relationships, clear lines must be drawn, and employees must be made to respect those boundaries.

The military is a place where young people are made to respect rules and authority. Military leaders create a follow-the-orders mentality because respecting the chain of command is a matter of life or death, especially during the chaos and confusion of battle.

In the movie *A Few Good Men*, a battle-hardened Colonel Nathan Jessep (Jack Nicholson) oversees the American presence at a dangerous base in Cuba. Jessep, called to testify in a murder trial, is on the witness stand talking about orders when he turns the interrogation around and asks questions to the prosecuting attorney (Lieutenant Daniel Kaffee, played by Tom Cruise).

"Ever put your life in another man's hands, asked him to put his life in yours?"

"No, sir."

"We follow orders, son. We follow orders or people die. It's that simple. Are we clear?"

"Yes, sir."

"Are we clear?"

"Crystal."

That testimony, of course, comes back to haunt the colonel because it was his orders that led to the murder of a soldier. This tells us something about the responsibility that comes with a position of authority—a position that can and should command respect. We can't take it lightly. And if we abuse our authority, we should expect to pay the consequences.

In fact, I'll make clear what I hope, but can't assume, would be obvious: no one needs or should employ workers who act as robots, marching only in the direction we tell them, never questioning policies or decisions. That's why initiative is a key factor in a strong work ethic. And if a boss abuses (or attempts to abuse) his authority, a worker needs to take a stand.

Initiative isn't so much breaking the rule that says "respect your boss" as it is proactively confronting a situation, even when the boss or a friend is breaking the rules. So now we're also talking about integrity. And professionalism. These things all work together; they aren't silos built miles and miles apart.

In most instances, there is no reason young people— or older workers, for that matter—must sacrifice their individualism or their ingenuity, much less their integrity, in order to toe the line for the organization that employs them. Conformity and obedience have their place. Indeed, most religions make obedience a central tenet—some out of fear, some as a response to love. And much like love, respect is a condition you can't order someone to adopt—it has to come from within.

Instilling Respect: A Real-World Scenario

After presenting the keynote for the annual meeting of the general managers of Ripley's Believe It or Not! museums, one GM lamented the difficulty she was having getting her young team members to comply with her "no cell phone on the job" rule. She told me that she needed all of her employees ready to engage guests and always looking to enhance the experience. Texting had become a major distraction for her young employees, and it was affecting her bottom line.

If an employee knows he's not supposed to text his friends while he's at work and does it anyway, he's cheating. He's not valued, nor is he adding value. If his manager leaves and things are slow, then he'll likely see no harm in touching base with a friend to check on plans for later that evening or to offer his opinion on the movie he saw the night before. As a skilled multitasker, he may feel he can even text while waiting on a customer—as long as the boss isn't looking and the customer doesn't notice.

If—or when—the boss discovers this lack of respect playing itself out in the employee, she might issue a verbal warning. "This is against company policy," she'll say. "Don't let it happen again." But it does happen again, because the employee rebels against what he sees as a stupid rule. "I can text and still do my work," he decides. "And what's the harm anyway, especially when things are slow around here?"

Then come written warnings, suspensions, and, if it keeps up, a pink slip.

The employee leaves bitter and frustrated. "Bunch of control freaks," he tweets as he mentions your company by name. His boss, meanwhile, begins her search for a new employee with lowered expectations for what she'll get. "Can I just find someone who can follow a few simple rules?" she tells a friend over coffee.

There are authors and experts who preach what I call the Gospel of Giving In. They suggest that employers should work to understand how these young employees think and feel, as well as why they think and feel that way. Once we understand all of this, the theory goes, we can accept these workers for who they are and play to their strengths. But don't ask them to change—that might hurt their self-esteem; just embrace who they are. In other words, eliminate the no-texting rule or just look the other way.

That's preposterous.

If your rule is outdated, get rid of it. But if there are valid reasons behind your rules and policies, you've got to establish respect for them. Besides, you're not doing your employees any favors when you allow them to challenge your standards. Your goal shouldn't be to accommodate the fact that these workers simply don't respect company policies, their coworkers, their supervisors, or their customers. Instead, your goal should be to help them see the value of respecting rules and how this makes them more valuable to the company. Regardless of how pervasive the "break all the rules" message has become in our society, employees need to understand that all of us ultimately have to respect rules and follow procedures with which we don't agree.

To put this concept into action, let's apply it to the texting-at-work issue that plagues many employers today. This is how I advised the manager from Ripley's to deal with this situation and move her cheating texters into the Valued Quadrant.

1. Clarify the expectation up front. Any new hire should be made aware that cell phone use on the job is strictly forbidden, or permissible only on breaks. If texting is a small issue, don't sweat it. However, if it's a huge problem, it's too important to leave for after the employee has accepted the job. Instead, it should be brought up in the first interview: "We don't allow cell phone use of any kind on company time. Some employees think this is unfair. What are your thoughts on this rule? Can you convince me that I'll never have to have a discussion with you about this?"

You *can* teach old dogs new tricks; in fact, you'll have to. Your rule isn't going to apply only to new hires—you'll need everyone to comply, or it won't seem fair and it's not going to last. At some point, you'll have to hold a company meeting to announce the rule and any consequences you're prepared to enforce, or you'll have to call your employees in one at a time to explain the new policy in detail. You may even want each employee to sign a memorandum of understanding so you won't have to deal with a lot of "I didn't know" excuses. It's not easy creating a new rule or enforcing an old one that's been abused for some time, but it is possible, and it starts with clarity.

2. Establish the rule's relevance. Getting employees to stop texting is simple if they know you are watching them on surveillance cameras 24/7. That's not realistic, though, and you're going to need them to buy into the rule when you're not around. So explain the reasoning behind your rule, and be prepared to back it up statistically or, at least, anecdotally. "You see, Emma, in an effort to remain a tourist's favorite attraction, we're always surveying our guests to find out how we can improve. The biggest criticism by far has been directed at employees who use their phones while they are on the exhibit floor. It ruins the experience for the very people who keep us in business. That's why we've made it a policy to disallow cell phone use of any kind by any employee while on the floor."

3. Mentor employees throughout the process. They may understand the rule and even the reasoning behind it, but you've just shut the world off to your young employee and he's going to need help and support. Here's where mentoring comes into play. In the following situation, notice how imperative it is to lead by example:

"Here's what works for me," you might say to the newly deprived employee. "I let my family know that I am off the grid between the hours of 1:00 and 9:00 p.m. on work days, and that if an emergency arises, they can reach me at the box office by leaving a message. I tell them the message has to be detailed, rather than just a 'Call home,' so I can better gauge the urgency. Then, during my breaks, I grab my phone and check my non-urgent messages and quickly reply to a few. I deal with all the social stuff when I'm off the clock. I don't keep my cell phone with me when I'm on the floor, and this alleviates all the temptation that comes with it."

4. Reward Compliance. You know what to do if you catch them breaking the rule, don't you? Write 'em up, issue a warning, send 'em home, or terminate them. The question then becomes whether you are equally prepared to reward compliance.

> "In the past, a leader was a boss. Today's leaders must be partners with their people . . . They no longer can lead solely based on positional power."
> —Ken Blanchard

This could take shape through your acknowledgement of an individual's respect for this rule during his thirty-, sixty-, or ninety-day performance evaluation by simply thanking him for being a team player and for prioritizing customer service above personal wants. On a grander scale, you could create positive peer compliance by scheduling celebrations for ninety days without a cell-phone-rule infraction and providing doughnuts, pizza, or just a big group thank-you at a team meeting. This focuses attention on the importance of the rule and allows you to restate the rationale behind it and the benefits your customers and your business receive when everyone complies.

Respect for You, Their Boss

Most experts agree that respect ultimately comes from

one of two primary emotions—love or fear. The thing to avoid is hate. You can get someone to do what you want if you have authority over him, even if he hates you, but that person won't respect you. And if he doesn't respect you, you can't trust him.

In *The Prince*, the classic treatise on politics originally published in 1513, Niccolò Machiavelli wrote that if someone had to pick between leading from fear or love, it's better to be feared than loved. That might have been true in his day, but it's hard to make an argument for that in Western culture today. The emerging workforce wants and needs rules and boundaries, but it doesn't respond well to fear-mongering managers.

Respect blossoms from well-nurtured relationships that are rooted in love, not fear. So the most important thing any leader can do when it comes to cultivating respect is to provide examples of respect. Display a respectful, sacrificial character—be positive, trust others, be polite, listen, be reliable, obey the rules, show mercy. In short, love others, and the people around you will respect you for it.

Fight the urge to demand their respect. Unless they're in a life-and-death situation, you're not going to get it. Instead, treat them with the same degree of respect you'd like from them, and your actions will be mirrored. At the same time, don't let their definition of respect become yours. You are the boss and are in control. They know that, and they'll respect you more for not immediately caving in to their demands. Instead, lead by example. They won't automatically respect you because you are older or because you have an important title attached to your name.

The good news is that your younger workers respect authenticity, accomplishment, and competence. If you have a strong personality, let it out. They have strong personalities too, and they are very tolerant of other people's differences. Remember, though, that they can spot a phony in a heartbeat. If you are naturally quiet, then demonstrate to them that you know what you're doing based on experience. When they learn what you did to get where you are—and they see your hard work and character shine through—you will earn their respect.

ADDITIONAL CONVERSATION STARTERS AND TIPS FOR INSTILLING RESPECT

A teenage worker at a call center might see it as no big deal to show up fifteen minutes late for work, until she realizes that her tardiness forced another worker—a single mother—to stay late, which made her late to pick up her son from daycare, which meant she had to pay a late fee, which meant she was going to have a hard time paying the rent that month.

Explaining rules and policies helps shatter the "me bubble," especially when you put a human face on the reasons behind the rules and the consequences of breaking them. Providing clarity and relevance is often all an emerging worker needs to buy into your rules.

When workers acquire respect—first a healthy self-respect, and then respect for the rules and their coworkers—they internalize a component of work ethic that drives every decision they make. That breathes life and energy into their ideas and actions, and it lays the foundation for success—immediately and for years to come.

The following are a few questions and prompts to get you started:

- What are ten rules that you would create for doing your job?

- Pick five rules you don't understand or agree with and try to come up with the reasons you think someone else thought they were needed.

- If you were the boss, tell me some things you would consider unacceptable behavior (a) in the way your employees treat you, (b) in the way your employees treat each other, and (c) in the way your employees treat customers.

- What personal benefits do you think come from showing respect for your work? For your boss? For your coworkers? For your customers?

- How do you handle conflict with others, and how do you think a focused, intentional respect for others might shape that?

- What's your favorite movie, and how did you see respect played out between the characters?

- What things have you been in charge of at home or at school that made you feel respected? Why?

- Tell me about a time when you felt disrespected by someone. What was that like? What was your response? How would you have preferred that person to have acted?

- Someday you will be in a position to manage others. Not everyone is going to like you and accept your authority. How will you handle those who don't?

- What will you do when you are in a position that requires you to enforce a rule or a policy with which you don't personally agree?

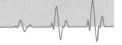

Universal Sandbox Values	Employers Want	Work Ethic Markers
Play nice, smile, and be polite	Positive, enthusiastic people	Positive Attitude
Be prompt	who show up on time	Reliability
Look your best	dressed and prepared properly	Professionalism
Do your best	go out of their way to add value/do more than required	Initiative
Obey the rules	play by the rules	Respect
Tell the truth	**are honest**	**Integrity**
Say *please* and *thank you*	give cheerful, friendly service	Gratitude

CHAPTER 10

INTEGRITY

"Character cannot be developed in ease and quiet. Only through experience of trial and suffering can the soul be strengthened, ambition inspired, and success achieved."
—*Helen Keller*

The crisis of faith for Professor Richard Quinn came in the fall of 2010 when he realized students in his senior-level business class had cheated on an exam.

Students cheating on tests isn't new, of course. It's enough of a problem in American colleges, in fact, that the University of Central Florida, where Quinn teaches, uses casino-like security cameras in its testing centers. The school has a national reputation for aggressively preventing cheating.

Professor Quinn might be a tad idealistic, but he's not naïve enough to think students would never attempt to cheat on one of his exams. What really hurt him was the number of cheaters on this particular test. Using statistical analysis, Quinn confirmed that two hundred of his six hundred students had cheated. One-third of the class—at a school that works hard to prevent cheating!

"I've always helped my students any way I could," Quinn said in an interview with ABC News. "And this was just like a knife through the heart."

Quinn gave an emotional speech to his class after learning of the rampant dishonesty. He told them the discovery had made him "physically ill. Absolutely disgusted. Completely disillusioned." And then he told them that all six hundred would have to retake the test. He knew who had cheated, he said, and the cheaters could confess and take an ethics seminar or risk expulsion.

The ABC News report also featured interviews with two students, one who saw the cheating as a travesty and another who saw it as no big deal. We don't know how many other students shared the view of Konstantin Ravvin, but his comments were even more alarming and discouraging than the percentage of cheaters Professor Quinn caught.

"This is college," Ravvin said. "Everyone cheats. Everyone cheats in life in general. I think you'd be hard pressed to find anyone in this testing lab who hasn't cheated on an exam. They're making a witch hunt out of absolutely nothing, as if it were to teach us some kind of moral lesson."[5]

It's Too Easy to Point the Finger

This morning before I wrote this chapter of the book, my wife and I went to a large retailer to pick up a gift for a family member. We arrived early, found the item quickly,

---

5   "University of Central Florida Cheating Scandal Prompts Professor to Issue Ultimatum," by Yunji de Nies and Karen Russo, ABC News, November 10, 2010.

and proceeded to check out. Ahead of us we saw a middle-aged mother, her twenty-year-old daughter, and the cashier, who was about forty (I'm guessing at the ages).

Cashiers for this national chain are likely given incentives each time they can convince a shopper to fill out a short credit application and charge their purchase to their new account. This particular cashier was telling the daughter that she could "save an additional 10 percent on their purchase by applying for the card on the spot—with approval in sixty seconds or less." To expedite the procedure, the cashier informed the woman that she could easily input all of this data using the point-of-purchase credit card terminal in front of her.

"All you need to do is enter your address, your date of birth, your Social Security number, and your annual income," the cashier says.

"I'm a student," the young shopper replies. "Outside of a few odd jobs, I don't really have an annual income."

"Oh, just put in $5,000," her mother instructs.

"No, that's not nearly high enough. Make it $37,000," the cashier advises.

"$37,000! But I'm basically an unemployed college student!"

"Don't worry. They never check," responds the cashier.

Mom adds, "Yeah, just do what the man suggests."

My wife and I look at each other in total disbelief.

It's not only harsh to point the finger at youth whenever we speak about the absence of honesty and integrity in this world; it's also inaccurate. After all, doesn't their behavior mirror their biggest influences?

At some point early in our lives, most of us hear, at least once if not many, many times, a version of an old

English proverb that goes something like this: cheaters never prosper.

The problem with that proverb, of course, is that it isn't true. Cheaters prosper all the time. Cheaters take a risk that very often pays off in a fast-lane ticket to significant prosperity.

O.J. Simpson avoids jail time despite considerable evidence against him in a murder trial. Alex Rodriguez confesses to using steroids but keeps on earning millions of dollars playing professional baseball. After repeated arrests for alcohol and drug related matters, Paris Hilton is apprehended for drug possession and found with cocaine in her purse. She denies the purse is hers and avoids jail time, but later claims the cash and credit cards in the purse do belong to her.

Celebrities lie and cheat their way to the top, and then lie and cheat to stay there. They're not alone. Businesses cut corners, advertise false claims, and present fraudulent images, all en route to greater and greater profits. Some get caught. Some get exposed. Some get punished.

Others don't.

Consider billionaire Armand Hammer, who died in 1990 at the age of ninety-two. Hammer was celebrated throughout his life as an iconic international businessman with a stellar reputation. He had been a personal adviser to several U.S. presidents. He had kept company with everyone from Charles, Prince of Wales, to Soviet Union leaders like Lenin, Brezhnev, and Gorbachev. He had spent much of his life flying around the world collecting art and crafting business deals that made him one of the wealthiest men on the planet.

But as Edward Epstein chronicles in his 1996 book *Dossier: The Secret History of Armand Hammer*, very little about Hammer's public persona matched his real-life character. Turns out, Hammer funneled money into a Soviet spy network, bribed politicians, fathered and then abandoned several children with several mistresses, sold phony art to unsuspecting clients, and twice let his father go to jail for crimes he committed.

Or, on a lighter note, consider Häagen-Dazs ice cream. You see the name and you think it's imported from somewhere in Europe, right? The early labels for the ice cream, in fact, included a map of Denmark. But founder Reuben Mattus and his wife Rose made up the name after spending hours at his kitchen table sounding out nonsensical words in search of a combination that would evoke a certain Scandinavian feel. Mattus might have been born in Poland, but his ice cream was and is fully American.

This marketing ploy, along with the fact that the ice cream is darn tasty, helped Mattus build a brand that he sold in 1983 to the Pillsbury Company for $70 million. Looks like the lines between clever marketing and cheating are pretty fuzzy.

Cheaters never prosper?

That proverb is a lie. And no amount of repeating it changes what we know firsthand from experience or from simply watching the world spin around us.

This begs the question, if you can elude the consequences of being dishonest and actually prosper as a direct result of dishonesty, why should you take a more difficult path to getting what you want?

> "In the old days, words like *sin* and *Satan* had a moral certitude. Today, they're replaced with self-help jargon, words like *dysfunction* and *antisocial behavior,* discouraging any responsibility for one's actions."
> —Don Henley of The Eagles

That question, in fact, speaks to the greatest source of pain experienced by leaders, managers, parents, and educators. When we invest our lives into someone else and that person betrays our trust—whether it's our own child, a student, or an employee—that betrayal feels, as Professor Quinn so aptly put it, "like a knife through the heart."

Integrity is a fundamental tenant taught in most major religions around the world. After centuries of neglect, however, we've become a culture that talks about honesty and integrity but lives it out less and less. This erosion of a core value—of doing what's right for its own sake and of living for a purpose larger than self—is affecting each and every one of us in profound ways.

Integrity as the Foundation of Your Business

In chapter 2, I mentioned that I had researched the markers of work ethic by asking hundreds of managers what they were looking for in employees and what they expected from them on the job. The summary sentence provided—"Employers are searching for positive, enthusiastic people who show up for work on time, who are dressed and prepared properly, who go out of their way to add value and do more than what's required of them, who will play by the rules, who are honest, and who will give cheerful, friendly service regardless of the situation"—is accurate. However, the seven specific markers that comprise this sentence are not listed in the order in which they were most typically given. When asked what they wanted and expected in each and every employee, the first word uttered by the largest number of respondents was *honest*.

Running a business becomes extremely difficult—if not impossible—when the trust between owners and management, or between management and the frontline, is lost. When you can't trust your employees, you're in deep trouble. But the reverse is equally true. When your employees feel as though they can't trust you, your effectiveness as a leader is minimal, at best.

Unfortunately, trust for you and your organization isn't something young people instinctively bring to the job. Many have been "burned" by the less-than-honest words and actions of previous employers, and if they haven't been, they know friends who have. Others have seen their parents downsized and outsourced by the very companies they sacrificed everything to help build. Throughout their adolescence, all of them have been conned, manipulated, cheated, and exploited by false media claims, bogus offers, and marketing ploys, leaving them leery of anyone who wants to use them to make a profit. Quite simply, your young workers enter your workplace wary and wise, with a giant B.S. detector glued to their foreheads. One business owner told me he feels like each new young employee makes him feel like he's a batter in the bottom of the ninth with the bases loaded and a full count. "I've got to be very careful of anything I say because every word is being scrutinized and analyzed," he said.

The Hole Truth

Dictionaries speak of integrity first as an adherence to a moral code or values, because that's how integrity plays itself out. But the secondary definitions speak to the greater truth, because they go back to the root of the word—a "wholeness" or "perfect condition" (c.1450). When we lack integrity, we're missing something. Our imperfections rule our lives. There is a "hole" in our character. When we live with integrity, there is a wholeness about us, a completeness of character that allows others to trust us unconditionally.

Our actions—one at a time—constitute our behaviors, and our character is the sum of our behaviors (public and private) over a period of time. So what drives those behaviors and defines our character? Integrity, or, in some cases, a lack thereof.

In 2009, the Josephson Institute of Ethics released a significant, large-scale study that gives great insights into the state of integrity. The California-based institute has long been doing biennial reports tracking the ethics of American high school students, but the 2009 study went deeper, gathering information from nearly seven thousand respondents in five age groups, from teens through retirees. It showed the strong connection between the attitudes and behaviors of the young with regard to honesty and the patterns of dishonesty as young people find their way into adulthood.

The institute's press release on the survey summed up the major findings in three bullet points:

- "The hole in the moral ozone seems to be getting bigger—each new generation is more likely to lie and cheat than the preceding one.
- "Young people are much more cynical than their elders—they are considerably more likely to believe that it is necessary to lie or cheat in order to succeed. Those who believe dishonesty is necessary are more likely to actually lie and cheat.
- "Cheaters in high school are far more likely as adults to lie to their spouses, customers, and employers and to cheat on expense reports and insurance claims."[6]

The study provides convincing evidence that Ravvin, the UCF student who spoke so bluntly in support of cheating, isn't some lone, radical voice. What we have in America is an ever-increasing tendency to see lying and cheating as inevitable and acceptable behaviors, which in turn creates a cycle of dishonesty that's nearly impossible to reverse. Everyone lies and everyone cheats; therefore, everyone must lie and everyone must cheat; therefore, I must lie and I must cheat, which means I become part of the pattern others see when they confirm the fact that everyone lies and everyone cheats, which, of course, leads them to lie and to cheat.

---

6 "Character Study Reveals Predictors of Lying and Cheating," Josephson Institute, October 29, 2009.

And so it goes. But as it goes, we all want one exception: *Sure, everyone does it and we all have to do it to some degree, but don't lie and cheat in your dealings with me. When you deal with me, I'd appreciate very much if you'd flip the trend and treat me with honesty and integrity.*

This is a blatant double standard, and I don't know anyone who isn't guilty of applying it. Members of the emerging workforce, like the rest of us, aren't surprised if big business and big government fail to treat us honestly and fairly, but they think they should. They expect their friends to be faithful and true. They expect their employer to pay them fairly and on time and offer a range of benefits. But they drive seventy-eight miles per hour when the speed limit is seventy. They use their job at the pizza parlor to give their friends a free pizza, and then explain the missing pizza as a botched order. They don't correct the cashier if she gives them too much change or rings up an item at too low a price. They repeat gossip about their friends when they aren't sure if it's true. They embellish their resumes. They take the answers someone found for the midterm and use them to improve their grade. They do some or all of these things and rationalize them. And *they* isn't confined to young employees; we all share in this to some degree.

That's what puts our workers—and us, if we're not careful—in the Cheating Quadrant. They know the rules, but they don't live by them. They engage in dishonest and immoral behaviors, and they put themselves on a slippery slope that takes them toward bigger and more damaging betrayals. Because if anyone spends enough time in the Cheating Quadrant (publicly or privately), it starts to feel like home and begins to define his character.

Living Integrity

I'm going to make an assumption—a sweeping generalization, actually—and I don't see it as a huge risk. I believe most readers of this book embrace integrity as a vital goal for daily living. In other words, I believe you, dear reader, are a person of integrity and a person committed to integrity. You fail at times because you're human, but living with integrity is important to you. It's important to you personally, and it's important to how you run your business. Not only that, but you think it's important to instill this value in the workers you hire and manage, not just because you want them to be honest when working for you, but because you want them to be successful people of character in all walks of life.

So you're looking at the emerging workforce around you and wondering how you can get people who see nothing wrong with cheating to rise up, commit to live with integrity, and find peace in the Valued Quadrant.

How can you help lift them over and up, into the upper-right quadrant, where they will best serve your interests and build their own value? How can you help them feel the pride they can only experience by choosing the difficult right over the easy wrong?

They first need be cognizant of what integrity is, what it looks like in your business, and why you surround yourself with it by choosing to do business with only those vendors, suppliers, clients, friends, and associates who personify uncompromising integrity.

How much time should you devote to conversations centered around trust, integrity, and honesty? As much as possible. You can't hire someone and think, *I know you've been raised to know right from wrong. And since you already know right from wrong, my job is merely to enforce it.* Instilling integrity takes coaching, teaching, mentoring—and a lot of it. Your workers need to know that you're the exception in the midst of a crazy world where it seems everyone is lying and cheating to get what they want.

Members of the emerging workforce will not always recognize integrity when they see it. They might see you facing a decision and notice that you went right when left appeared easier. And they might assume you're just not very smart. Everyone cheats, right? And yet you passed up the easy path for the more difficult one. They don't see this as an act of integrity, but rather frame it as the act of some old fogy who isn't hip to the way things are done.

That's why you need to look for the teachable moments you can use to bring clarity not just to the rules and policies of the organization, but also to the reasons behind your decisions.

You might say, "Vendor A was 12 percent less expensive than Vendor B, but Vendor A wanted a kickback. While this might be appealing to some, it's a practice that goes against what we stand for. We won't do business with anyone that we can't trust, even if it means paying a higher price."

Or, "We could enter this code in the software and use unlicensed versions on several additional computers, but that's not the way we operate. We would be cheating that company out of revenue it deserves. We don't want our customers to rip us off, so we don't cheat the system."

On the flip side, if you act in ways that display a lack of integrity, personally or corporately, young workers will see that as par for the course, and they'll use those cracks in your character to justify their own dishonesty. It's confirmation of their belief that everyone cheats—on their taxes, on their exams, and in business. Imagine how that worldview will be shattered when they discover that you're different.

From Personal Honesty to Cultural Integrity and Back

You can't overcommunicate integrity on the front end, but talking about it is not enough. You need to call attention to it when you see it, recognize it, reward it, and celebrate it so that it radiates throughout your organization. Seems over-the-top, but it's not.

I'm certainly not suggesting that you need to give an employee a $20 gift card to the Gap because she found a $10 bill on the floor and returned it to the rightful owner. But acknowledging and celebrating integrity as a worthy value helps create a culture that lives it, expects it, and expresses it. So look for those golden moments when someone takes responsibility for a problem when he didn't have to fess up, or when someone puts a hard truth ahead of an easy lie. Look for ways to honor those acts of integrity. Tell the person privately and, when appropriate, celebrate it with your team.

You also can celebrate where you want an employee to go. When a person's been on the job for a few weeks, you can encourage and empower her by saying something like, "I'm really glad you're on our team because I need people I can trust, people who will do what they say. I need people with great character." Give your workers something to live up to, a reputation they can embrace, and the feeling that you think of them as trustworthy.

These suggestions help build cognizance and compliance, but integrity is a process that's driven by deep, internal values. Anyone can commit random acts of integrity. They can find themselves in the Lucky Quadrant from time to time. Or they can intentionally do what's right occasionally just to put on a good front and cover for their more significant deceits.

Real integrity becomes part of a person's operating system. Real integrity requires a buy-in and commitment that's from the heart, not just the head.

You can help inspire that with encouraging words and by rewarding and recognizing integrity in the workplace. But to really get buy-in from the emerging workforce, you have to help these individuals value trust and honesty in a world that appears to promote and even celebrate the opposite.

How?

First, ditch the punitive. Scare tactics don't work with the emerging workforce. These workers know that the odds of you filing charges against them are slim, because they know how much time and money

> "I am personally convinced that one person can be a change catalyst, a 'transformer' in any situation, any organization. Such an individual is yeast that can leaven an entire loaf. It requires vision, initiative, patience, respect, persistence, courage, and faith to be a transforming leader."
> —Stephen R. Covey

that will cost you. If you do prosecute them, they know that even if you can prove your case, they'll probably get off with a slap on the wrist. They aren't easily scared by threats, and you don't want people who are only honest because they're afraid of getting caught. That doesn't mean you shouldn't clearly communicate consequences. And by all means, you should enforce those clearly communicated policies. But don't think punishments or the threat of punishment will significantly affect the behaviors of the emerging workforce.

Second, you have to trust them. It's hard, especially when you go back and read the statistics I quoted earlier in this chapter that indicate that this generation of workers by and large sees cheating and lying as acceptable. But this generation hates to be micromanaged. If you clearly describe your expectations and set high standards, but then constantly look over workers' shoulders, they will quickly feel like you don't trust them. This will likely make them live down to your expectations. You need checks and balances that protect your business, but give employees a chance to earn your trust. Start with small things and move forward. The greatest way to build trust in a young person is to show him that you trust him.

Third, and this is the biggie, you have to pull employees out of their "me first" bubbles and let them see how dishonesty affects both people around them and their own personal peace. For example, a young employee might think that hooking his buddy up with a free soft drink isn't really an integrity issue. He's been told that fountain drinks are a high-profit item and that it only costs the company a couple of cents for the syrup and the cup. He thinks, "This company makes millions, so it's not going to miss a few pennies here and there." He's thinking of himself, his friends, and his reputation, and he doesn't see the connection between his behavior and the real cost to anyone outside his bubble.

This is where a leader can make a tremendous difference. By understanding the mentality, she can make certain her people know the real cost of the fountain drink—well beyond the cost of the ingredients—and share with them how heavily the company relies on every cent to keep people employed and maintain growth. She can also let them know that prices rise when waste of any kind occurs.

Granted, a three-minute lesson like this isn't going to dramatically alter the behavior of anyone and transform a dishonest kid into a boy scout, but it will go a long way toward removing some of the rationalizations the kid might be using to justify his actions. From that point forward, he will be forced to at the very least consider how his actions might adversely affect his company, his boss, his coworkers, and even his peace of mind. He'll no longer be able to brush off this seemingly simple act of dishonesty as "no big deal."

What Happens in Vegas . . . Affects All of Us

Great leaders are well aware that young people are being hit from all sides with messages promoting dishonesty and irresponsible behavior. So they hit them every bit as hard with messages that celebrate honesty and integrity, showcasing people (often other employees) who are committed to doing the right thing, who are making a positive impact, and who are trusted and respected by others.

Yes, cheaters often prosper. But even though you can't convince today's young workers that they'll never be able to get away with it, you can convince them that they'll never get away from themselves. Wherever they go, they'll eventually have to make peace with the person in the mirror.

That reminds me of a poem I learned back when I was eleven. My mom found it reprinted in a "Dear Abby" column in the Sunday paper, and she cut it out and pasted it to my mirror. This happened a few days after she'd confronted me with a lie that I had told her and thought I'd gotten away with. Here it is in its original, unedited form.

The Guy in the Glass
Dale Wimbrow, 1934

When you get what you want in your struggle for pelf
And the world makes you King for a day,
Then go to the mirror and look at yourself,
And see what that guy has to say.

For it isn't your Father, or Mother, or Wife,
Who judgement upon you must pass.
The feller whose verdict counts most in your life
Is the guy staring back from the glass.

He's the feller to please, never mind all the rest,
For he's with you clear up to the end,

And you've passed your most dangerous, difficult test
If the guy in the glass is your friend.

You may be like Jack Horner and "chisel" a plum,
And think you're a wonderful guy,
But the man in the glass says you're only a bum
If you can't look him straight in the eye.

You can fool the whole world down the pathway of years,
And get pats on the back as you pass,
But your final reward will be heartache and tears
If you've cheated the guy in the glass.

ADDITIONAL CONVERSATION STARTERS AND TIPS FOR INSTILLING INTEGRITY

My training company once gathered eighteen leading high school and college educators and asked them to come up with some ways to teach honesty in the classroom. At the heart of their ideas was the need to create meaningful discussions about the topic.

So, for instance, they suggested that a teacher put a $20 bill on her desk and then leave the room. A student would have the assignment of taking the money off her desk while she was out. When she returned and asked about the missing money, she would have the perfect opening for a discussion about honesty.

- Why isn't anyone talking?

- If you know who took it but don't want to rat on him or her, are you doing the person a favor, or me a disservice? Or are you just being a coward?

Once you explain what's going on, the discussion can move to more general topics.

- What's the cost of dishonesty?
- What happens when you get ripped off?
- If the person who took it gets away with it, how is he or she going to feel tonight? How are you going to feel tonight?

Your Example Is Showing

Here's how you can set you and your organization apart from the others, while at the same time creating undying loyalty with your frontline workers: tell the truth. Nothing will win their respect and admiration like honesty. Aim for 100 percent truth, 100 percent of the time. Because they find it so rarely, truth works like a magnet to attract young people and helps you to earn their unshakable confidence and trust.

Before you say anything to them, first ask yourself, "Is this true?" Step back and take a look at all of your communication with them. Do you ever make promises you can't keep? Are any of the standards for satisfactory performance hidden? Are empty threats made as a scare tactic? Are the promises of raises and promotions exaggerated?

Do your employees feel the need to embellish stories just to get a point across or to feel like they're being heard?

If your answer to any of these questions is yes, it's time to reevaluate your relationship with your employees. Your young workers won't commit their talents to any person or organization that has tried to mislead or exploit them, and once it's happened, they'll rarely give the offender a second chance.

Remember, their eyes are upon you. You can't allow yourself—or anyone in your company—to indicate that things are anything other than 100 percent ethical and above board. You can't be "kind of honest," just as a woman can't be "kind of pregnant." Always model the highest standards of honesty, character, and integrity with customers, vendors, employees, and your up-line managers, executives, and stockholders.

Here are a few dialogue starters:

- Have you ever had anything of yours taken from you by a dishonest person? How did this experience make you feel?

- What would you do if you studied hard for a test and found out that someone next to you was cheating off your paper?

- What's the difference between squealing on someone and reporting a serious crime?

- If you owned your own restaurant, boutique, electronics store, etc., and you found out a key employee had been pilfering just a few small items from you every once in a while, how would you react?

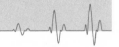

■ ■ ■

Universal Sandbox Values	Employers Want	Work Ethic Markers
Play nice, smile, and be polite	Positive, enthusiastic people	Positive Attitude
Be prompt	who show up on time	Reliability
Look your best	dressed and prepared properly	Professionalism
Do your best	go out of their way to add value/do more than required	Initiative
Obey the rules	play by the rules	Respect
Tell the truth	are honest	Integrity
Say *please* and *thank you*	give cheerful, friendly service	Gratitude

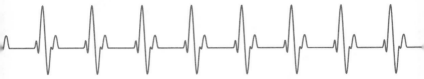

CHAPTER 11

GRATITUDE

"A customer is the most important visitor on our premises; he is not dependent on us. We are dependent on him. He is not an interruption in our work. He is the purpose of it. He is not an outsider in our business. He is part of it. We are not doing him a favor by serving him. He is doing us a favor by giving us an opportunity to do so."
—*Mahatma Ghandi*

Imagine for a moment that you wake up one January morning shivering from the cold. As you rub the sleep from your eyes, you look around and slowly realize that all your worldly possessions are gone. Vanished. You are on a cot in an open field in an arctic climate; your warm bed and safe home are nowhere in sight. You have a thin blanket and no pillow. You are wearing old socks, shoes, underwear, pants, and a T-shirt. You are hungry. Your joints ache. And you are alone.

You sit there for ten or fifteen minutes considering this reality. You are in shock. You literally pinch yourself to make sure it's not a dream. It's not. It's real. You are scared, angry, and confused. Then you start to think about what you're going to do. Snow from a dark, gray sky begins falling around you. Where will you get food? How will you stay warm? What about your loved ones? Are they safe? Are they warm?

As you take all of this in, you close your eyes for a few minutes to think or pray.

When you open your eyes again, all of your stuff is back. You are sitting in your king-size bed with fresh sheets and a down comforter. Heated air flows through the vents in your bedroom, where you sit within insulated walls that are covered with a shingled roof. Clothes fill your dressers and walk-in closet, and there's a television across the room hooked to a cable that feeds it a few hundred channels. You smell fresh coffee brewing and cinnamon rolls baking in the kitchen downstairs.

You shake your head as you look around. You don't know how or why you experienced what you just did, and it really doesn't matter. You have a completely different perspective than you experienced the previous morning. Everything has changed. You're not thinking about what you have to do, or what you want, and you're certainly not thinking about anything you don't have. Nope. Today you're feeling a deep, profound appreciation for the life you now live and everything in it.

Compared to your typical morning, how would you approach the breakfast table? How would you interact with your family? How would you feel about your job, your boss, your coworkers, and the customers you serve?

If you threw yourself into this imaginary scenario, I would wager that you'd be feeling enormous gratitude, and that even if you were a gifted actor, you couldn't conceal that feeling from anyone around you.

And what does this scenario have to do with work ethic? Everything.

I began our discussion about the components of work ethic with positive attitude, and I'm ending it with gratitude. We've come full circle, so much so, in fact, that it's hard to say which really comes first.

Gratitude, of course, is an attitude, and gratitude helps us create and sustain a positive attitude. Likewise, when we approach life with a positive attitude, we inevitably give thanks for the things around us. It's that thankfulness that we express as gratitude. Each feeds the other.

> "As we express our gratitude, we must never forget that the highest appreciation is not to utter words, but to live by them."
> —John Fitzgerald Kennedy

The two things, however, aren't the same, and that's why it's worthwhile to examine them separately for their roles in developing work ethic.

You might recall that I defined your attitude as a choice you make about how you will view life, including work. Gratitude, likewise, is a choice you make, but it's specific to thankfulness. Perhaps even more essential to the distinction, it's a choice to make a selfless expression of thankfulness.

Gratitude isn't passive. If it becomes passive, it quickly dies. If you can't see it, it really isn't there. And it can't be self-focused, or it becomes diluted and discolored—a cheapened version of the real thing. When it's real, however, it generates more of itself.

> "Gratitude is a quality similar to electricity: it must be produced and discharged and used up in order to exist at all."
> —William Faulkner

Where work ethic thrives, gratitude shines. And where gratitude shines, work ethic thrives. That's because work ethic without gratitude is just work. It's a robot performing tasks that get accomplished but that lack their fullness, their greatest value. Gratitude produces loyal, content workers and loyal, satisfied customers. It not only gets the job done, it gets it done in ways that drive down turnover and drive up repeat business.

Gratitude and Your New Workforce

Abraham Maslow's famed hierarchy of needs states that beyond our basic survival needs, all humans beings have the desire to be accepted and valued by others. People engage themselves to gain recognition and have activities that give them a sense of contribution. We want to know that we count, that we matter, and that we belong. The pain that comes with feeling ignored, unappreciated, or being taken for granted can be crippling, and it certainly disconnects us from others.

Your young employees have grown up differently and are wired differently, but they haven't reshaped Maslow's triangle. They live to know that they matter, and they want to know that they are an important part of your present success and future plans, whether or not you are a part of theirs. They've been dubbed "feedback junkies" and "praise addicts" because they have a deep-seated desire to know that they are doing good work and that they are valued.

Why then, you might ask, when they crave positive affirmation at an almost insatiable level, are they so stingy with gratitude and positive affirmations for others? Why won't they show the same level of appreciation they demand from their boss and their job? And why don't we see them pulling out all the stops to unselfishly attend to the needs of your customers and express the kind of gratitude that ensures those customers return to do business with you again and again?

Let's examine three sides to the problem, followed by some solutions.

1. IT'S ALL ABOUT ME

The world gives a nod and a wink in the direction of gratitude, but it never stops begging us to ask one overriding question: "Are you paying attention to me?"

Think about the messaging youth has received from today's entertainers and athletes, who, like it or not, are their role models. Celebrities are in the business of drawing attention to themselves and promoting their star power. In an age where the media has become saturated with entertainers, anyone that wants to get noticed has to out-yell, out-brag, and out-promote his peers. These individuals may have a few seconds to say nice things about the director, the producer, and the cast, but they know that if they don't quickly refocus the spotlight on themselves, their chances for making headlines are diminished.

In the NFL, players (and their agents) demand payment based primarily on key statistics like yards gained and touchdowns scored. Those are important, of course, but championships are won with blocking and tackling, and champions are made of teams that serve the greater goal by serving each other. The quarterback can't complete touchdown passes if the linemen don't block. And the quarterback who isn't grateful for a good offensive line quickly loses the linemen's loyalties and, in some cases, their protection. After the game, a few occasionally credit their team, but most work in their numbers and stats so voters will not forget them when they mark their all-star team ballots. More attention always equals more money. And with money, you can buy more attention.

This braggart syndrome isn't something that's confined to the rich and famous. I'm not a celebrity or a professional athlete, but my personal brand matters greatly to my success. I make my living mostly by speaking to groups of people. I also write books and run a company that provides youth work ethic training to schools and leading companies and organizations. And no matter how much I believe that my messages are more important than I am, the reality is that I still have to self-promote to generate business. I have to tell people I am a good speaker, a good consultant, a good writer, and so on. If I took a much more modest approach and said to an interested meeting planner, "Well, there are a whole lot of speakers out there who are better than I am. But if you think I'm up for the task, I'll give it the good old college try," they'd politely dismiss themselves and go call someone else. So where do you draw the line between confidence and overstating your case?

In this media-saturated world, marketing, advertising, and PR machines drive us to focus all of our attention on the winner, the champ, the numero uno. And the more we—and the emerging workforce—see celebrities and athletes push and shove to get in the spotlight, the more we lose sight of the others around us. We feel the need to scream louder and promote harder than our competitor or we risk losing business. We've got to talk about us and repeat our awards, statistics, and credentials. It's no longer enough to show self-confidence; we're often left in the position of having to lift ourselves *at the expense* of others rather than *with gratitude* for others.

Your young employees have been raised in a culture in which modesty and humbleness are endangered, if not extinct. And when an individual's focus is on self, he can't possibly put the customer's needs first.

2. THE PRICE OF GRATITUDE EXCEEDS THEIR VIEW

I recently shared a platform with Frances Frei, Professor of Service Management at Harvard University. Dr. Frei has done extensive research in the science of customer service and turned the lights on for the executives at this particular leadership summit when she told us that brands that want to excel at good customer service have to be intentionally bad at some other aspect of their business. Discount retailers, for example, go to extremes to be great at offering low prices, but they are intentionally bad at customer service. However, their customers forgive them because they know they are trading great price for bad service. The Ritz-Carlton, on the other hand, provides exceptional customer service, but is intentionally bad at price and The Ritz-Carlton's customers forgive it, too.

I'd always known this at some level, but Dr. Frei's clarity of this point got me thinking. Go with me on this . . .

As a general rule, where are your young employees more likely to shop: Nordstrom or Target? Where do they dine more frequently: Morton's or McDonald's? Where do they have their oil changed: Jiffy Lube or the Lexus dealership? When they travel, where do they stay: the Ritz or the Super 8?

If it's true that you can only give away what you first own, how can they give great service when their life's experience has been comprised primarily of bad service, self service, or no service? How can we expect them to go out of their way for your customers when the majority of their own purchases have been made with the click of a mouse? How can they show unselfish gratitude when they've never really owned it, at least from the perspective of a customer?

The fact is, they can't.

It doesn't mean that they're physically or mentally unable to provide great service; it only means that expressing gratitude and providing excellent service is not inherently a part of their DNA.

3. FEELING ISOLATED, DISCONNECTED, AND UNIMPORTANT

A third reason your young employees are not prone to expressing gratitude is that they don't see themselves as being as vital to your business as they really are. *You* realize that they are the face of your brand, but they don't know what that means, and they don't feel the weight of the responsibility that comes with it.

"I just ring up sales and drop groceries in a bag," a young supermarket cashier said to me recently. "A monkey could do this job. In fact, they've got self-service registers right over there, so unless you're really lazy or really dumb, why the hell would anyone want to wait in line over here?"

How tragic. This young lady had no idea why I was in her lane. Perhaps her manager should have told her that many people chose her lane simply because they wanted more than a faceless digital transaction and a thank-you from a computerized voice. Shoppers often choose a live cashier over a machine not because they don't know how to use the interface, but because they're looking for a break from technology. They want to engage with a friendly face. Like me, those who chose this cashier's lane quickly discovered their error in reasoning. Because of her, some won't return.

Statistics from the U.S. Department of Labor show that the number-one reason people leave their jobs is that they don't feel appreciated. They feel they don't count, and that they don't matter. Turnover is a problem, to be sure, but the bigger problem is when your frontline people mentally leave their jobs but forget to tell you—and remain on your payroll as the face of your brand. When this occurs, all their internal feelings of disconnection and lack of importance get rolled into a giant wad of apathy left at the foot of your customer. Do you think the cashier at the supermarket felt appreciated? Do you think she thought her job was an important one?

The words your employees use can be a telling sign of how they see their roles. Employee engagement expert Mark Scharenbroich points to the increasing frequency of the response "No problem" as an indicator of how many frontline employees view serving others as an accident or an unwarranted favor rather than their intent and their primary purpose.

"Thanks for the pizza!"

"*No problem.*"

"Thank you for getting me in to see Dr. Muldoon so quickly."

"*No problem.*"

"Thanks for selling us our dream home!"

"*No problem.*"

No problem? What about, "It's our pleasure to bring hot, tasty food to your door," or, "We're honored that you have chosen Dr. Muldoon as your dentist"?

Serving others can be one of the most gratifying things we do, but it needs to be done in the spirit of self-lessness, joy, and gratitude. And that's only going to occur when workers have internalized the fact that they do play a pivotal role in your business, and that when they go out of their way for your customer, they do make a difference and a ripple that exceeds far beyond your P&L.

Problems Are Good Things to Have

You need your employees to show gratitude in all phases of their job, right? It doesn't matter whether you're operating a fast-food restaurant, a high-end retail shop, a grocery store, a law firm, a bank, or a hospital—you want them to solve problems for your business and for your customers, and to take pride in the process. A valued employee understands that his job exists to solve problems, and he doesn't run away from them but toward them. For example:

Your problem: you need someone who will work the cash register. Your customer's problem: she needs to check out quickly, get full credit for her coupons, and know that she's paying the correct prices and getting the correct change.

Your problem: you need doctors who will be on-call during the night shift. Your customer's problem: he needs help at 1 a.m. for his three-year-old son who has a 101-degree temperature.

Your problem: you need people in sales who deliver new business. Your customer's problem: he needs a dependable router that will operate correctly, last a long time, and get serviced quickly if it stops working.

You have problems—or maybe you call them challenges or opportunities. You bring other people onto your team in the belief that they will solve those problems in ways that generate revenue and repeat business.

So how does gratitude solve problems?

Remember earlier when I argued that gratitude is active rather than passive? That it is lived out as an *expression* of work ethic that *produces* something? That it is a selfless action, not just a feeling? Well, gratitude leads directly to the type of problem-solving customer service that sustains a business.

If your workers are grateful, they will care about their coworkers, their employees, their boss, your company, and your customers. And if they care about those things, they will do all they can to help each of them succeed—to help solve their problems.

If they don't care—if they are living without gratitude—they become passive. They don't think about others, much less how to help them solve their problems.

My son, Zac, worked his way through college as a sales associate for a multinational wireless phone provider in one of the company's bigger retail stores. Customers who came into this store fell into one of two categories: those who were purchasing phones, accessories, and service plans, and those who were seeking help, repair, or refunds on the products and services they had already purchased.

Zac and the other sales associates in this retail store were paid a base salary, but their real earning power came from commissions paid on new product sales. Whenever Zac activated a new service plan for a customer, he'd get a nifty bonus on his paycheck. But if it was his turn to wait on a customer, and that particular customer already had a phone and only needed help downloading a ringtone or setting up an e-mail account, Zac would have to spend fifteen to thirty minutes solving their problems, for which he received no additional commission or bonus. He'd tell me that other sales associates would look past anyone who looked like they already had a phone and approach only those who appeared to be phone shopping.

This particular wireless giant spent hundreds of millions of dollars on attracting new customers, but how successful do you think it was at retaining its existing customers? Not very. The key to success for this company was clearly not in the quality or frequency of ads it aired, but rather the gratitude its sales associates showed for the company's existing customers when those customers had a problem.

The truth is, customer service is abundant when there's a direct benefit to the employee—a pay incentive, a tip, or a bonus—for providing it. But you want your employees to show gratitude—to smile, to say *thank you*, to enthusiastically look for solutions to the customer's problems—even when there's no apparent kickback. And that's where your role as a leader and mentor takes hold.

Inspiring Gratitude

When the Grinch stole Christmas from all the Whos down in Whoville, he lacked a basic understanding of the spirit behind the holiday. The scrawny-limbed hermit with a nasty attitude and a foul grimace hated the world and everything in it, and he wanted everything and everyone to share in his misery. Of course, it was rumored that his heart was two sizes too small.

So what changed him?

Well, the good Dr. Seuss made the moral quite clear: the Grinch had to see for himself that Christmas wasn't about things, but about giving, loving, and caring.

You might have a Grinch or two working for you. They don't solve many problems; in fact, they create them. Why? Because they lack gratitude—for their work, for the company, for their coworkers, for their boss, and for their customers.

Unfortunately, you can't teach them gratitude. You can define it for them and tell them they need to be grateful. You can tell them to smile and say *thank you* and be nice to customers and coworkers. But, much like respect, they need to embrace gratitude internally to make it last and to make it truly effective.

To do this, you still start with increasing cognizance. You can't assume that the emerging workforce arrives with an understanding of what gratitude is or what it looks like—especially in ways that are specific to your team and organization. So you have to assess each employee's understanding of the concept. What were their experiences before joining your team? What do they already know, or not know, about being part of a team? Have they been thankful for previous jobs, or do they take jabs at previous employers? Have they lived with or worked with people who were committed to getting better every day? Do they thank you for your time, write a thank-you note for the interview, and thank you when they leave? Are they smiling as if all of their material possessions had mysteriously vanished—and then magically returned? Never underestimate the significance of hiring smiling, happy people who exude gratitude.

As a leader, you must make certain your people know what gratitude means to you and your organization. You have to describe the policies and procedures, and teach them the expected corporate culture. The more they understand the scope of your business and their role in bringing customers back, the less likely they'll be to feel lost, insignificant, and unimportant. They'll worry less about immediate results and more about the ultimate results—the long-term results that really matter.

With you as a tour guide to show them the bigger picture, they begin to understand that solving a customer's problem with her cell phone might not lead to an immediate activation that triggers a financial reward for them, but that it does improve their personal reputations and the store's reputation. This, in turn, increases traffic and increases opportunities for many new sales. Some of those sales might go to other associates, but as the saying goes, a rising tide lifts all boats, and they'll have a flood of new opportunities if others also go out of their way to solve problems.

Meanwhile, Back at the Rock . . .

Let's go back to my friends at Hard Rock. Take a look at Hard Rock's four corporate mottos—"Love All—Serve All," "Take Time to Be Kind," "All Is One," and "Save the Planet." Those all sound swell, don't they? But the muscle behind them comes from the way the organization lives them out.

"Our culture is only created by doing the things we say we're going to do," Jim Knight, director of the School of Hard Rocks, told me.

Hard Rock holds all sorts of philanthropic events throughout the year to support worthy causes, and very often the management teams are serving elbow-to-elbow with hourly employees. Some of their events, in fact, are led entirely by employee groups. They also have a variety of policies that promote things like recycling and energy efficiency. And every single initiative on the company's marketing calendar includes a philanthropic tie.

Over time, the employees in the emerging workforce see that companies like this really do stand for something bigger than themselves. And the employees want to live for something bigger than themselves. They want to help others and save the planet, so now they feel like they are in part doing that by working hard each day and helping the company succeed. The company's commitment feeds its employees' desires to do good in the world, and the fruit is a positive attitude and gratitude, resulting in problem solving and great customer service.

"They want to do meaningful work, and they're going to make socially conscious work and spending decisions," Knight said of Hard Rock employees. "They want to belong to a cause bigger than themselves and work for a company that cares about giving back and leaving a smaller footprint in the world."

When gratitude lives among individual leaders and within an organization, most employees will see it, respect it, and embrace it. The few who don't can and should move on, but the ones who do will become the best on your team. They will attack every task with a sense of gratitude, and that gratitude will shine in the work they do.

This should be the difference between employing a person rather than a vending machine that merely takes the money, dispenses a product, and gives change. Personal customer service begins and ends with gratitude. It actively says, "I'm glad you chose my lane. I want to affect your day and put a smile on your face. I'm going to do whatever it takes to make sure your problem is solved. I'm glad you're here, even if I don't get a nickel for serving you, because I want you to come back and tell your friends." And the "you" in that dialogue, by the way, is anyone other than "me"—it's the boss, the customer, the coworker, the community, the business.

These are the ultimate deliverables of gratitude—that the employee rolls up his sleeves and serves others, that he's dedicated to making sure the customer is elated, that he solves problems. He seldom, if ever, says, "I'm doing these things out of gratitude"—he just does them. When he's giving thanks for the things around him, he'll give great service to everyone around him. That's gratitude in action.

ADDITIONAL CONVERSATION STARTERS AND TIPS FOR INSTILLING GRATITUDE

Gratitude, like almost any positive trait we hope to see in others, is best taught by example. So, the way you express your appreciation for your work, for your customers, for your employees, and for your business all play a central role in helping develop a sense of gratitude in the workers you employ.

It should go without saying, but I've seen too many managers complaining out loud about their work to assume that everyone understands and lives out this principle. True leaders are humble, but confident encouragers. They aren't prideful, and they don't complain to their troops.

Instilling gratitude requires expressing gratitude in front of your people and for your people. So look for opportunities to tell them that they matter, and that you appreciate their work. Don't do this collectively. Don't praise a room full of people at a company meeting by broadcasting a quick "You're all doing a good job." Rather, look for specific instances when you can call out an individual for the good work she's doing and thank her for what she's done, specifically mentioning why she deserves praise. When employees see you notice, they will start to notice others. When you care for them, they will care for themselves, your company, and your customers.

Radiate gratitude in your culture by looking for opportunities to engage employees in conversations about things like their role in the big picture of the business, how they view customer service, how they see their gratitude for coworkers, and how and why they exceed customers' expectations.

Here are a few dialogue starters:

- How does dealing with customers and coworkers help you grow as a person?
- How can you exceed customers' expectations?
- What do you expect from workers when you go into other businesses?
- Tell me about a time when someone went above and

beyond your expectations. How did that make you feel about that person? About that establishment?

- What are your barriers to expressing gratitude? What are some ways you can overcome those?

- Who do you know who is both humble and confident? What do you like about being around that person? What role do you think gratitude plays in that person's approach to work and life?

- Tell me about a time when you dealt with a rude, difficult, or demanding customer who you wanted to give up on, but hung on with only to end up winning them over.

- If everything you owned was suddenly vaporized, leaving you with absolutely nothing, what would you do? If it suddenly rematerialized fifteen minutes later, how would you react? If you're that happy about what you already possess, remind yourself how fortunate you are each day before you come to work, and your grateful attitude toward others will come back to you tenfold!

Finally, look for teachable moments. Inevitably, we all deal with people and situations that make it hard to show appreciation. When that happens, we take action or we don't; we fail or we succeed. When failure happens, encourage employees to talk about it.

When an employee faces a difficult customer or sees you deal with one of them, take some time later to talk about the types of solutions—poor, average, or great—that were used or could have been used.

CHAPTER 12

The Valued Proposition

If you think multitasking is a modern phenomenon—a skill somehow mystically implanted into the DNA of Generations X and Y—then you probably don't remember Erich Brenn.

Brenn built a career by showing off his multitasking abilities to audiences around Europe, but he really hit the big time in America in the 1960s with recurring guest appearances on *The Ed Sullivan Show*. He would come onstage dressed in a tuxedo and stand in front of a table covered with plates, bowls, sticks, trays, glasses, spoons, and eggs. Then, with Khachaturian's high-energy "Sabre Dance" playing as background music and the studio audience watching in wonder, he would go to work putting everything on the table into motion.

By the end of his act, he had five glass bowls spinning atop four-foot-long sticks, while eight plates were spinning on the table below. Brenn would also do things like flip the spoons into the glasses or swoop a tray from beneath the eggs so they would fall perfectly into the glasses on a tray below them. All this while working frantically to get—and keep—all the plates and bowls spinning.

Watching plate-spinners like Brenn perform reminds me of leading the emerging workforce: it never ends.

The best leaders, of course, manage their time and energy so that life isn't always so frantic. These leaders establish priorities and delegate responsibilities; they understand the healing value of rest and the importance of knowing how many plates they can effectively spin at the same time. But make no mistake: signing up for leadership—especially if you're leading the emerging workforce—means signing up for some plate-spinning. Some times are less frantic than others, but there are always plates or bowls that need spinning. You can't spin them once and expect them to spin forever; it isn't a once-and-done task. And so it is with leadership—especially with the daunting task of reviving work ethic and restoring pride in the workplace.

> "I took my dog for a walk—all the way from New York to Florida. I said to him, 'There, now you're done.'"
> —Comedian Steven Wright

We can't teach members of the emerging workforce the values of work ethic and then simply sit back and watch as they go about blazing a new trail that changes the world. Some will become masters of it and go on to teach it to others around them, but not without time and practice on their part and patience and persistence on your part. Even if some of the people you lead become experts in work ethic, they'll always need help staying in the Valued Quadrant. We all do. Plus, there are always newcomers joining the team—more workers from the ever-changing emerging workforce.

As a leader, you have to do your plate-spinning with a purpose and with the right number of plates. All the people I know who embrace the call of leadership do so in part, usually in large part, because they enjoy the challenges and rewards that come from helping others move forward. They like the feeling of purpose that comes with spinning these plates.

As we near the end of this book—this discussion about reviving work ethic—we need to keep in mind that we're not going to breathe life into the emerging workforce and then ride off into the sunset. We're starting a process. Each day brings new challenges and opportunities. Your young workers have grown up in a different world, one that is constantly prodding them to look for ways to separate effort from reward. They may not see much value in having a good work ethic. Heck, they might not even see the value in having values.

That's why you must never stop assessing the progress of your employees. You can never stop clarifying your expectations. You can't stop mentoring. In other words, you can never stop moving young workers across the horizontal line of cognizance—moving them to the right, from "don't know" to "know."

Likewise, you can never stop motivating and inspiring compliance—lifting them up from "don't do" to "do." You must continue to search for ways to prove that the values you hold sacred are both relevant and timeless, and you must become an expert in how to reward those who demonstrate these values in your workplace and radiate them throughout your culture.

Up and over.

Over and up.

We want to bring these individuals into the Valued Quadrant and help them stay there so that they, in turn, can help others. That's why we spin these plates.

Connecting

Have you ever gone to the store to pick up some batteries for your flashlight and walked out with batteries, some chips, a candy bar, and a six-pack of cola?

(Okay, so maybe the six-pack wasn't cola.)

Why? Probably because some advertising or marketing professionals "helped" you realize your need to purchase their products. A radio ad that you heard in the car planted a seed as you drove to the market, or an in-store display grabbed your attention as you passed through an aisle, or the tech gurus managing your favorite brand texted you a special offer on your phone as you walked in the door of the store. Whatever it was, it nudged you toward a certain product that then went into your basket, through the checkout line, and made its way home with you.

In short, you bought what they were selling.

When you look at the emerging workforce and think through all the things they need to learn about work ethic—the seven values, in particular—you can start by asking yourself a simple question: *what will get them to buy what I'm selling?*

You see, if they think *you* are the one who wins when they buy in, you're never gonna close the sale. They've got to feel that you have *their* best interests at heart—that you want them to win as they work for you, and even after they leave.

Hopefully, you do want them to succeed regardless of where they end up. If you don't, they'll see that you're only trying to manipulate them and they'll display these values only when you're watching. Instilling these timeless values isn't something you can do with a selfish heart. Your primary objective must be to make them better in every way, regardless of where the road ahead leads them.

Achieving results at this level with the emerging workforce isn't easy, and I believe it's nearly impossible with training alone. That's not a knock on training—hey, I own and lead a company that trains the emerging workforce! Training is vital! But that training must work in concert with coaching and mentoring.

William Mayes, senior vice president of sales and marketing for Senior Home Care, hires regularly from the emerging workforce. His sales team includes around two hundred people, and many of the new hires are in their twenties. They have worked part-time jobs, made it through college, and had success with one, maybe even two, previous full-time jobs. And they have, or can quickly learn, the skills needed for success as sales reps on Mayes's team. A few have the kind of work ethic required for success with this growing company, but Mayes will readily admit that many don't. As he points out, "Even when we find the people who *can* do the job, we don't know if they *will*."

So Mayes often meets personally with young hires or connects them to one of the veteran sales reps for some work on the values that are important to their organization. "We coach them and mentor them and give them extra time and attention," Mayes told me.

That time and attention requires focus, however. This is where the business of work ethic gets very personal. It's where you start connecting with the emerging workforce to find ways that help them align their personal needs and expectations with the greater good of the organization. It's where you discover the value propositions that an individual and an organization can share.

"We need them to buy in to what we're doing," Mayes says. "The turnover rate in sales is 50 percent, so we have to find ways to keep them engaged. And it's not about them. It's about us. We have to get them to understand the 'we' mentality."

Realistically, however, Mayes knows you can't just tell new young hires that it's all about the team and expect them to fall in line. You have to help them get there—from wherever they are.

"We have to meet them where they are," Mayes explains. "Everyone has goals. We have to help them get where they want to go. Our job is to motivate them while they're working that plan. It's a lot of effort. That's the whole challenge."

There were times when the boss simply laid down the law to the employees, and the employees, usually out of fear of losing their jobs, went along. If they went along for long enough, they learned to appreciate the values. As Mayes and so many other leaders have discovered, that strategy seldom works in today's marketplace.

"You can't motivate people by fear," he says. "They don't have fear in their hearts. You have to figure out where they are, what they feel, what matters to them, and then tie things together. Let's make it happen together—meeting them where they are and giving them a reason to move where they want to go, and where we want to go."

This type of connecting builds the work ethic you need in your employees. And in doing so, it shifts their mindsets away from a utilitarian view of work. When that happens, loyalty increases and turnover decreases.

Five Strategies for Mentoring

I've offered some practical tips throughout this book on instilling the values that make up work ethic, and most of those tips have to do with building relationships that allow you to speak to and influence the lives of members of the emerging workforce.

Those tips generally fall into one of several strategies for mentoring young people. You probably picked up on most of these themes, but I'll summarize them here to help you as you strive to move young people into the Valued Quadrant.

1. Find your style. This won't come as a shock to you, but you aren't me. Not only are you not me, you aren't anyone else but yourself. So you have to figure out how to personally apply the truths you've come across in this book as you connect with your emerging workforce. You have to personalize the message.

Sounds simplistic, but we tend to forget this from time to time. Emulate others when it makes sense and fits your personality. If you aren't sure about your style, start with the advice of C.S. Lewis: "The way for a person to develop a style is (a) to know exactly what he wants to say, and (b) to be sure he is saying exactly that." If you start there, you will at least know you're going in the right direction.

2. Develop trust. Connecting takes time, especially with the emerging workforce. Many of these young workers arrive with suspicions about your motives, or they are so self-focused that they hardly know you exist, much less that you are a human worthy of trust.

To develop trust, ask questions and listen to what they have to say with an empathetic ear. You don't have to fix all their problems, but you need to care—and *show* that you care. Then look for opportunities to relate your life experiences to theirs. Don't interrupt them over and over to tell your war stories, but giving them some insight into your life can go a long way.

You should have an agenda, but you lose trust when it seems like all your words and actions are focused on your agenda and nothing else. If your agenda *includes* understanding and helping your members of the emerging workforce grow and improve, then they will respect you as a leader and buy into your values and your vision.

The well-researched book *Influencer* (by Kerry Patterson, Joseph Grenny, David Maxfield, Ron McMillan, and Al Switzler) put it this way: "You must replace judgment with empathy, and lectures with questions. If you do so, you gain influence. The instant you stop trying to impose your agenda on others, you eliminate the fight for control."

And think about it: trust is the first casualty in any fight for control.

3. Value tact and timing. Knowing when to address issues and doing so in the right ways is often the difference between success or failure in communicating with the emerging workforce (or anyone else).

The key, I believe, is not rushing into meaningful conversations. Even if you have to address something immediately, try to at least take a breath before charging into the situation. Even praise needs to come with tact and timing. Think it through. Have a plan. Make it count.

When you want to encourage a value, notice it in a specific action or behavior and immediately call attention to it. "You've been early every day this week, Miguel. I can rely on you, and that really matters to me." "Sarah, when someone says something as offensive to you as what I just saw from that patient, and you don't lower yourself to their level but rise above it to focus on the solution, you raise the level of service here for everyone else. I'm so thrilled we have you at the front desk to greet patients and solve problems!"

Conversely, when you see someone acting out in a way that is contrary to one of these values, pull him aside and let him know in private. Resist the temptation to approach him in anger, and avoid attacking him. Instead, ask him to explain the situation from his perspective. Then ask if he thinks it should have been handled differently. Clearly explain your expectations, and ask whether he thinks he can meet them the next time and how he's going to rise to the challenge.

4. Tell stories. The emerging workforce was raised on narratives. These individuals relate to and learn from good stories, so it behooves managers to develop their storytelling skills.

Some things to keep in mind are as follows:

- Make sure your stories have a purpose. Don't just fill the air with the sound of your voice.

- Remember the attention span of your audience and keep your stories short. Know where you're going before you leave, and get to your point in a few minutes or less.

- Deliver stories that have an impact, and make the delivery unique and engaging. This requires thought and creativity on your part so that you can deliver something fresh that shocks them or entertains them, but ultimately enlightens them.

- Use technology cautiously. We all know that the emerging workforce eats, sleeps, and breathes technology, and that's exactly why you don't want to overuse it. In fact, most PowerPoints or multimedia presentations will seem lame to the emerging workforce. There are times when you can take a popular YouTube video or some other pop-culture experience and use it as a teaching tool. But in general, visual analogies tend to work more effectively when you're sharing a simple story to make a point. Paint them a word picture.

5. Cast a vision. You've heard this one before many times, and yet I believe most leaders need to rethink what this really means. We know all about casting a vision for the organization—"Here's what we want to look like in ten years" or "Here's where we want to go as a team." That's all well and good. But when we cast a vision for individuals, it all too often involves feeding them ego biscuits that actually cause more harm than good.

For years, we've praised children and young adults for how well they perform—in math, in science, in athletics, in music, in arts. Yet, studies now show that many students take this praise as a sign that they don't have to work hard. They're told they are great at whatever they've attempted; why try harder? So they only excel until they face a challenge, which they tend to avoid. Failure indicates they've tapped out their ability. Or, if they fail early on in any particular pursuit, they assume it's because they lack talent for it and therefore should try something else.

Jonathan Zimmerman, an educator for nearly thirty years who now teaches education and history at New York University, wrote about the impact of this mindset in a 2010 article for *The Christian Science Monitor*.

"Americans like to say that their country is a land of opportunity; that anyone can make it, if they just try hard enough," he wrote. "But our educational system tells another story altogether. By emphasizing who is smart—and who is not—we teach our kids that their inborn capabilities are more important than their sweat and toil."[7]

You can counteract this mentality by casting a vision and delivering praise that emphasizes the values we've touched on throughout this book, not just the results of supposed natural talent. Casting a vision for hard work gives them a foundation for excellence in nearly every endeavor. It takes the emphasis off the person's innate talent and puts it on the work it takes to refine and improve

---

7 "Why Shanghai schooled the US: Americans think they're too smart to work hard," by Jonathan Zimmerman, *The Christian Science Monitor*, December 14, 2010.

that talent. They might have some of that, too, but they won't excel until they learn to build it into something far greater than it was when they walked in your doorway.

When I speak with leaders across the country, whether they are in health-related industries, financial services, hospitality, or retail, I hear all sorts of stories about the challenges they face with employees in the emerging workforce. These individuals tell me what's worked, what's failed, and where they are running into brick walls as they search for solutions.

I've boiled down what I've learned from my clients' rich experiences and supplemented them with my own experiences and research. I've done my best to share my findings with my clients and with you in the pages of this book. I believe restoring work ethic values to the American workforce is essential to our country's long-term success. And I believe the best place to start this restoration project is with the emerging workforce. These people are our future.

So, if we can study, learn, and teach these values, and if we can put this knowledge into action in our lives and in the lives of our workers, then we can lift the emerging workforce and our entire economy up and over—into the Valued Quadrant.

NEED A TOOL FOR DEVELOPING THE WORK ETHIC IN YOUR ORGANZATION?

You need your employees to bring their very best to work every day. But if they haven't yet learned how to work, where can you turn?

Employers everywhere are hailing the *Bring Your A Game to Work* training and certification program as "the driver's license for the workplace."

The A Game's revolutionary training curriculum and online certification platform teaches, instills, and reinforces the seven core work ethic values every employer demands, giving young employees the knowledge and the confidence to succeed and to be proud of the work they do.

Here's how the critical seven essential work ethic values are alliterated in A Game-speak:

Employers Want	Reviving Work Ethic Markers	Bring Your Game Values
Positive, enthusiastic people	Positive Attitude	**A**ttitude
who show up on time	Reliability	**A**ttendance
dressed and prepared properly	Professionalism	**A**ppearance
go out of their way to add value/do more than required	Initiative	**A**mbition
play by the rules	Respect	**A**cceptance
are honest	Integrity	**A**ccountability
give cheerful, friendly service	Gratitude	**A**ppreciation

Find out how the A Game can help you increase productivity and performance and improve customer service in your business while reducing absenteeism and costly turnover.

Visit www.theAgame.com today or call 303-239-9999.